SAND TO SILICON

JEFFREY SAMPLER AND SAEB EIGNER

SAND TO SILICON

ACHIEVING RAPID GROWTH
LESSONS FROM DUBAI

P

PROFILE BOOKS

To our families and friends

First published in Great Britain in 2003 by
Profile Books Ltd
58A Hatton Garden
London ECIN 8LX
www.profilebooks.co.uk

3 5 7 9 10 8 6 4 2

Typeset in Minion by MacGuru Ltd
info@macguru.org.uk

Printed and bound by
Emirates Printing Press, Dubai

A CIP catalogue record for this book is available from the British Library.

ISBN 1 86197 627 5

Contents

Preface

In many ways this project is a microcosm of Dubai – people from different backgrounds and experiences working together to achieve something that would have been impossible without true collaboration and the merging of skills.

Saeb has extensive knowledge of the Middle East, especially the lower Gulf, and has been travelling there on business for some twenty years. Jeff has been visiting the Middle East region for the past few years to lecture at economic forums and corporate strategy events. Jeff's lack of familiarity with Dubai's history showed when he asked Saeb about a series of photographs he saw hanging on the wall of the Dubai Trade Centre Club, while attending a London Business School Alumni event.

The photos showed what appeared to be a small village of tents and mud huts, with a few traditional dhows moored in the muddy water of a modest creek alongside them. When Jeff discovered that the photos depicted Dubai not of a century ago, but of the 1950s, the degree of growth the area had experienced became immediately clear. Jeff shared his sense of astonishment with Saeb, and the two began to flesh out the building blocks of what would become *Sand to Silicon*.

The simple question that motivated this book – how was such growth achieved in such a short period of time? – proved to be the beginning of an extremely interesting quest. However, much like Dubai, the answer was more subtle than the obvious achievements that are visible to the naked eye. To help us understand these subtleties we were fortunate to have access to many of Dubai's leading businessmen and government officials. In the process, Jeff learned that Saeb's cell phone contains the telephone numbers of the 'Who's Who' of the region, and we were both humbled by the graciousness and time provided to us by many incredibly busy and important people, all of whom wanted the story told, as if it was their own. Such a sense of pride and achievement.

This kindness is perhaps best illustrated by our first interview with Dubai's visionary Crown Prince. His Highness General Sheikh Mohammed Bin Rashid Al Maktoum (who is referred to hereafter as Sheikh Mohammed, as he is more commonly known to everyone in Dubai). We were told it would be difficult to see him on this trip, but a few phone calls were placed while we were interviewing Mohammed Abdulla Al Gergawi, head of The Executive Office and Chairman of the Dubai Development and Investment Authority, and Sheikh Mohammed agreed to see us at his desert farm on a Saturday night. We were relieved that the meeting could take place early in our research, as how better to get the insights into an organization than talk with its CEO.

About an hour into the desert from central Dubai, we arrived at Sheikh Mohammed's retreat, where he keeps his cherished stable of Arabian endurance racehorses, many of which have been ridden to victory in international competitions by Sheikh Mohammed and his sons. We arrived just after sundown and were shown into a large trophy room displaying all manner of equestrian art, trophies, and photographs from competitions, where we waited patiently while Sheikh Mohammed finished his meeting with a prominent European CEO at the other end of the room. We expected a similar twenty-minute meeting, but once his other guests had left Sheikh Mohammed invited us to relax with him and have dinner around a great fire outside, under the stars.

We were shown to a bonfire surrounded by pillows and bolsters on Persian rugs. There we were joined by Sheikh Mohammed and two of his senior officials, Mohammed Al Gergawi and Sultan Bin Sulayem. We relaxed and talked long into the desert night. While we enjoyed the fresh-grilled lamb, flatbread and salad, Sheikh Mohammed answered our questions honestly and candidly, without any of the guardedness or detachment one might easily expect. He was genuinely interested in our book project and, to gain a solid understanding, asked thoughtful and probing questions.

By the end of the evening, we had completed an incredibly interesting interview with the man who many say is responsible for the exceptional success Dubai has been experiencing. But some of our most important insights from the evening had nothing to do with what was spoken around the fire. We experienced first-hand the remarkable presence of the Crown Prince that seems to affect nearly every area of everyday life and work in Dubai. His ability to make us feel at once welcome and relaxed while engaging us in an active, challenging dialogue was a unique experience that stayed with us throughout our visit. The interview truly helped us understand what nearly everyone we spoke to meant when they mentioned the leadership of Sheikh Mohammed.

What was evident was Sheikh Mohammed's energy, drive and total belief in what he is trying to achieve, albeit not at all costs. He naturally understands the need to balance Dubai's growth with its culture and traditions, and seems concerned that the social infrastructure keeps pace with his business vision – for without this balance he feels that the growth may be difficult to sustain at such a pace.

Indeed, these views of balanced growth were shared in many of our interviews outside of Dubai. For example, Sir Richard Branson (Chairman of the Virgin Group) and The Earl of Home, formerly David Douglas-Home (Chairman of Coutts bank, who was previously with merchant bank Morgan Grenfell, one of the early corporate financiers of Dubai) both spoke of how they admired Dubai's open approach to business. Sir Richard Branson was highly complimentary of Dubai's open sky policy. Both commented how, remarkably, business success had been achieved bearing in mind the additional worries and duties not normally the concern of a CEO, such as the social responsibilities of education, hospitals, infrastructure and the environment, to name but a few, including managing Dubai's role in the federation of seven emirates.

In our quest to capture the perspectives and efforts that have lead to the amazing growth and success of Dubai, we sought at the same time to develop a model for balanced corporate growth in which both business and social responsibilities work successfully together. Indeed, as business and its role in society evolves, this will be one of the main challenges to 21st century senior management. We think that Dubai provides a wealth of insights on these topics – and we hope that after reading this book you will do so too.

Acknowledgements

We'd like to begin by thanking Sheikh Mohammed, not only for the magical evening at his desert retreat but also for being so easily accessible thereafter. (The authors 'bumped into' him many times, the last being at a Starbucks in Dubai as one of the authors was having a coffee!) We could never have completed this project in such a short period of time (which we now refer to as 'Dubai time') without the help of many people, most of whom we hope to have listed here, but there are surely others, and our warmest thanks go to them as well. There are some who asked to remain anonymous and we have, of course, respected that wish and thank them too.

Our research was assisted by a vast array of government figures who generously shared their thoughts with us. They included Mohammed Ali Alabbar of Dubai's Department of Economic Development and Emaar Properties (among Dubai's leading organizations), Sultan Bin Sulayem of the Ports, Customs & Free Zone Corporation; Khalid Bin Sulayem of the Department of Tourism and Commerce Marketing; Khalid Al Kassim of the Department of Economic Development; Abdul Baset Al Janahi of the Dubai Development and Investment Authority; Ahmed Al Banna of the Dubai Chamber of Commerce and Industry; Charles Neil of the Dubai International Financial Centre (DIFC) and Essa Abdulfattah Kazim of the Dubai Financial Market. Emirates Bank International is another of Dubai's success stories, and we were fortunate to spend time with its CEO, Anis Al Jallaf, who is also chairman of the Dubai International Financial Centre and who had originally come up with the idea of launching the book in Dubai to coincide with the World Bank Governors meeting there, and Suresh Kumar of Emirates Financial Services.

There are many in Dubai who believe that the 'wave' of the future can be seen beyond the city centre, reaching to the Dubai Technology, Electronic Commerce and Media Free Zone. We are grateful to those who helped us gain a close understanding of this area, including the zone's Director General Ahmad Bin Byat and Abdulhamid Juma of Dubai Media City; to Tejari's Sheikha Lubna Al Qasimi ('Sheikha Lubna'), and Microsoft's Abdullatif Al Mulla, who provided the 'tenant company' perspective.

Travellers throughout the world who have yet to experience the delights of Dubai may have, nevertheless, passed through its stunning airport or flown on its world class airline, Emirates. Our profound thanks to those who provided perceptive thoughts into the challenges of maintaining and growing these facilities: Sheikh Ahmed Bin Saeed Al Maktoum ('Sheikh Ahmed'), President of Dubai's Department of Civil Aviation and Chairman of Emirates Group (which includes the airline); Maurice Flanagan, Group Managing Director of the Emirates Group (who is always so very generous with his time, never turning down a request); Mike Simon, the Director of Corporate Communications for the Emirates Group; Dr Mohammed Al Zarouni of the Dubai Airport Free Zone Authority; and Anita Mehra Homayoun, Director of Marketing at the Department of Civil Aviation.

We are also very grateful to representatives of the private sector who shared their perspectives with us, including: Abdulla Majed Al Ghurair of Bates PanGulf; Raja Easa Al Gurg of the Easa Saleh Al Gurg Group; Avi Bhojani of the Bates Group; Kito de Boer of McKinsey & Company; Ian Fairservice of Motivate Publishing; Teresa Farah of Habib Al Mulla & Company; Ziad A. Galadari of Galadari & Associates; Shehab Gargash of Daman Securities; Mike Stevenson of PricewaterhouseCoopers; and Raja Trad of Leo Burnett MENA.

We also thank all at Jumeirah International in Dubai for looking after us so very well during our many stays at their splendid hotels.

In London, we are grateful to The Earl of Home for sharing his early experiences of Dubai since the 1960s; Geoffrey Bignell LVO for having kindly read and amended the introduction and who, too, knew the area during the early days. We are also immensely grateful to Dr Anwar Gargash, Executive Director of Gargash Enterprises and a well-known columnist, an invaluable source of local knowledge and a most generous friend in both his and his family's time, for giving us much logistical support and advice during our stay and for having read the introductory chapters of the book more than once. We should also like to thank the Honourable Apurv Bagri for arranging for the Singapore chapter to be read for us, Sir Richard Branson for his views on Dubai, and his group strategy director, Gordon McCallum, for having made that possible.

Also, many thanks to our friends and others in the region who have given their advice, time, and thoughts freely – providing a perspective of how Dubai is viewed by its neighbours.

Thanks too to Sarah Bond and our editor Stephen Brough, both of whom have made invaluable contributions in the final stages.

We are especially indebted to all those at The Executive Office of Sheikh Mohammed, including its Chief Executive Mohammed Al Gergawi and members of his team, Hafsa Al Ulama, Habib Mahlouji, Wafa Al Khatib and Ruby Dominic.

Very special thanks go to Andrew Conway, our tireless research assistant, whose flexibility, skill and efficiency made it possible for us to complete this project in 'Dubai time', and whose actual contribution extends far beyond mere research. Thanks too, of course, to all who have commented kindly on the book, some of whose comments are quoted on the jacket.

Finally, we would like to thank our families for their patience and support whilst we were immersed in the creation of this book compiled during our 'free' time over the past year, since we both otherwise have demanding day jobs.

1 Introduction

Our business story is about courage …

SHEIKH MOHAMMED

This is a book about Dubai and how the lessons of its successful, large-scale, rapid growth can be applied to corporations. Today it is almost impossible not to be aware of Dubai. Over just three generations and mostly within the past half century, this tiny emirate has raised its profile globally through a range of bold developments and clever ideas. These include free zones for business that have made it a regional centre for many firms, a biennial air show, Dubai International Airport, Emirates airline, Jebel Ali Port, the new Dubai International Financial Centre, the Dubai World Cup horse race, its development as a tourism centre with some of the most stunning hotels in the world, including the Burj Al Arab (the world's only 'seven-star' hotel), and the great variety of facilities to be made available on the Palm Islands development and those contained within the Burj Dubai (to be the world's tallest building).

Many attribute much of the emirate's recent growth to its being run like a corporation, hence the much used metaphor of Dubai Inc. Sheikh Mohammed and his father, His Highness the late Sheikh Rashid Bin Saeed Al Maktoum, before him, have been fond of saying that 'what's good for business is good for Dubai'. And the reverse is also true. The government's structure has more in common with that of a private-run company than a public one. The ruling family appoint senior government officials and, together, they start and manage most of the big initiatives in Dubai, while the government does step back when it judges the moment right to leave matters to market forces. Dubai's success owes a lot to its openness: it has opened itself to the world through its free zones and lines of communication and access from top to bottom and bottom to top are remarkably open. There is a strong bond between the people of Dubai and the ruling Al Maktoum family, and business is largely done on the basis of trust, with regulations introduced only when they are felt necessary to reinforce trust and confidence. Sheikh Mohammed runs a lean government machine and is loath to slow it and Dubai down by adding layers of what he considers (and many in Dubai tend to agree) to be unnecessary bureaucracy.

This book appears at an important time in Dubai's development. Its rapid growth shows no sign of slowing down, and some say that it is in danger of creating a bubble that can only end up bursting. They point to the endless construction of residential and commercial property and hotels, wondering if there can ever be demand for that much. Such scepticism is not new in Dubai: most projects undertaken by the government had their critics, when they were announced. But now that Dubai's global visibility is at an all-time high, the stakes are perhaps higher than ever before.

Chapter by chapter

In Chapter 2, a brief history of Dubai sets the stage and introduces the basic concepts behind its rapid growth.

Chapters 3 and 4 examine two models for growth: Silicon Valley and Singapore. Silicon Valley is a bottom-up, organic growth model, in which dynamic R&D and technology businesses have developed with little intervention since just before the Second World War. The growth of Singapore, by contrast, has been driven from the top down. Since the country became independent in 1965, Lee Kuan Yew's government has created a huge portfolio of projects designed to create a good standard of living for Singaporeans. Singapore is cited by many in Dubai as a source of inspiration and there are indeed many similarities between the two of them, from their early prosperity as entrepôts, the success of their government-owned airlines and other industries, to the recent excitement with high technology.

But despite the overt similarities, Dubai's growth model lies somewhere between Silicon Valley's bottom-up and Singapore's top-down approaches. Dubai is compared and contrasted to these models in Chapters 3 and 4, and the details of the Dubai model are examined in the following chapters.

Chapter 5 considers the first phase of what we have called the strategic trajectory model, which explains how Dubai has achieved its large-scale, rapid growth. Called the **asset creation** phase, it starts with the development of the Creek, which set the emirate off on a strategic trajectory, building on existing capabilities, which would continue over the following decades.

Chapter 6 examines the next phase: **asset acceleration**. Once Dubai had created a basic portfolio of assets – ports, airports, airline, manufacturing plants and so on – their utilization was ratcheted up several notches to act as a springboard for future asset creation – even greater shipping capacity, free zones, hotels and the creation of the Palm Islands. Each new asset helped build momentum.

Chapter 7 looks at the third phase: **asset leverage**. This is when all the components of the business ecosystem or strategic vortex combine to create further value. Increasing numbers of visitors and competition among hotels drive innovation and growth in the hospitality industry. The early success of Dubai Internet City, a high-tech industrial park, is attracting more companies from around the world and spawning similar free zone developments. Building on and reinforcing the assets that currently exist drives future development along the same strategic trajectory.

Chapter 8 moves on to **asset harvesting**, **reinvestment** and **reinvention**. This is the phase that closes the loop in the process. Assets that have outlived their usefulness can be harvested and their resources redeployed (returning to the asset creation stage). Assets that continue to be useful and productive may need reinvestment. Others may need adjustment, closing down or reinvention to maintain their momentum, or completely new ventures may spring out of established ones.

Lastly, Chapter 9 considers what lessons can be drawn from Dubai's success and applied to corporations and other organizations.

2 Dubai in perspective

What is good for business is good for Dubai.

SHEIKH RASHID

There are many spots to sample the contrasts of modern Dubai. There's the Gold Souk, no longer an open-air market but a seemingly endless row of storefronts selling all manner of jewellery and trinkets made from the metal that's been a mainstay of the local economy for decades. There's a walkway alongside Dubai's Creek, where traditional dhows moor in the shadow of gleaming skyscrapers. Or there's the track at Nad Al Sheba, home of the world's richest horse race.

But probably the best vantage point to take in all that is modern Dubai is the lobby of the Emirates Towers hotel and its adjoining office and shopping complex. Usually buzzing with activity, it mirrors the bustling business environment in Dubai and the diversity of the people who do business there. Some wear traditional Middle-Eastern dress, though most are in Western business or casual attire. While English and Arabic predominate, numerous other languages are spoken. Most people are likely to be involved in trade or services rather than oil-related transactions, as oil now accounts for less than 10 percent of gross domestic product (GDP).[1] (See Appendix 2 and Appendix 4.)

There will also be many women, both UAE nationals in traditional dress and foreigners, including some wearing risqué fashions. Women are free to work, drive and come and go as they please in Dubai with no fear of harassment. It is not only in business that Dubai enjoys more liberal attitudes than other parts of the region.

From the lounge on the 50th floor of the Emirates Towers hotel can be seen the sail-shaped Burj Al Arab hotel built on its own man-made island. Perhaps the emirate's best-known landmark, as a result of the marketing of Dubai as a tourism destination, its image also graces every Dubai licence plate. Also visible is the constant flow of cargo into Port Rashid, a reminder of the trade that has underpinned much of Dubai's growth. In the foreground, the view from the bar includes the high-rise hotels, apartment buildings and offices along Sheikh Zayed Road constructed in the past decade. Many have helipads in anticipation of things to come. Adjacent to the hotel is the vast expanse of sand where the Dubai International Financial Centre is taking shape.

Behind the hotel, across the busy eight-lane Sheikh Zayed Road and high-rise glass buildings, are blocks of low-rise housing, some old, some new. A mosque is within walking distance of most dwellings, underlining the importance and prevalence of Islam in Dubai. As another indication of Dubai's diversity and tolerance, all this can be taken in with any chosen beverage, which is not an option in many states in the region.

Vital statistics

One of the seven emirates comprising the United Arab Emirates (UAE), Dubai lies on the eastern coast of the Arabian Peninsula. It covers 3,885 square kilometres, or 5 percent of the total land area of the UAE (excluding islands), although the majority of its population is concentrated in Dubai City. In terms of geographic size, it falls between Luxembourg and the US state of Delaware. Compared with Singapore, Dubai has less than a quarter of the population living in an area over five times larger. With its natural harbour opening into the Gulf and the Indian Ocean beyond and its location midway along major east-west and north-south shipping routes, Dubai has long been a regional trade centre. As traders and business people have been drawn to the area, both the population and economic output have grown markedly.

At the beginning of the 20th century, about 3,000 people lived in Dubai.[2] By 1947, the number had grown to 25,000.[3] In 1975, following the discovery of oil and the start of many large infrastructure projects, the population grew to 183,200. By the end of the century that number increased fivefold, reaching 910,300 in 2001.[4] (See Appendix 3.) Of this, fewer than 20 percent are UAE nationals, with expatriates from the Indian subcontinent making up the majority.[5]

In the last quarter of a century, Dubai's GDP has grown from $2.2 billion in 1975 to $17.5 billion in 2001 (at current prices).[6] At the same time, dependence on oil revenue has declined, from 46 percent of GDP to only 8.5 percent, and GDP per head has increased to over $19,000.[7] Thus Dubai has one of the highest GDPs per head in the world, providing its residents with a good standard of living. The government's goal is to increase GDP per head to $25,000 by 2010.[8] (See Appendix 2.)

To understand what lies behind this growth, it is helpful to look back at Dubai's history.

A brief history

Until 1833, the area now known as Dubai was inhabited by a few pearl divers and fishermen and their families living at the mouth of the Creek. That started to change with the arrival of an offshoot of the Bani Yas tribe from Abu Dhabi, the UAE's federal capital. Led by Sheikh Maktoum Bin Buti, the Al-Bufalasah group brought 800 new settlers to Dubai, and Sheikh Maktoum became the first of many Al Maktoum family rulers of Dubai. (See Appendix 1.)

Early traders
During the decades that followed an increasing amount of trade was attracted to the Creek, and by the end of the century many merchant families had prospered.

The growing importance of the region became apparent to the British, who, at that time, were not reluctant to establish footholds wherever they could to secure their shipping routes. Between 1820 and 1892, the rulers of Dubai, along with other Arab sheikhs, signed a series of treaties that gave the British increasing powers of policing and dispute arbitration. These agreements ensured safe passage along the shipping routes and prevented other powers from encroaching, while leaving internal rule to the sheikhs. Following the agreements of 1853, the area became known as the Trucial States, a name that would remain until the British withdrew in 1971.

At the end of the 19th century, Dubai's fortunes were boosted when many traders decided to forsake Lingah, the most prominent trading port in the lower Persian side of the Gulf, after new regulations and taxes were imposed. The then ruler of Dubai, Sheikh Maktoum Bin Hasher Al Maktoum, taking advantage of Lingah's decline, helped establish Dubai as an entrepôt and set a direction that Dubai has since followed. Persian merchants began to flock to Dubai, and merchants from elsewhere in the region followed. By 1906, there were around 2,000 houses around the Creek and 350 traders in the souk, making it one of the biggest in the region.

The depression of the late 1920s and 1930s, combined with competition from Japanese cultured pearls, sent the Dubai economy into decline. Trading continued nevertheless, with the gold trade as a mainstay. Determined as ever, Dubai's traders found in the period after India's independence a particularly lucrative market for grey-market goods among closed economies such as India, Pakistan and Iran.

But trade was hampered by the limitations of Dubai's natural infrastructure. By the 1950s, traffic in the Creek was almost at a standstill. The merchant ships and fishing vessels often had to moor three abreast, and silting reduced the width of the navigable lanes as well as their depth, which in places was only two feet.

A port and an airport

The traders who depended upon the Creek for their livelihood complained to the then ruler, Sheikh Rashid, who, mindful that infrastructural modernization of the Creek would enable new shipping companies with larger vessels to use Dubai, decided to proceed with a costly expansion project. It was a bold move; the projected cost represented several times Dubai's annual gross domestic product. To raise the necessary finance, a tax was imposed on imports; there was a bond issue, which was taken up by the major trading families who depended on the Creek; and Sheikh Rashid borrowed the remaining funds from the Emir of Kuwait, effectively mortgaging Dubai in the process.

With finance secured, the project went ahead in 1959 and was completed in 1960. As a result, trade increased by 20 percent to nearly $17 million (equivalent to about $103 million today). Furthermore, the income from import taxes enabled Dubai to repay its loan from Kuwait much earlier than expected.

The project provided Dubai with a much-needed boost in trading capacity, and set the tone for many more speculative projects. The Creek improvements were viewed with scepticism by others in the region, particularly in light of the risk posed by the loan arrangement with Kuwait. This scepticism would re-emerge many times over the coming years (indeed, you hear it even today) as similarly ambitious and risky projects were undertaken, and each time the government's gamble would pay off.

While the Creek was dredged and modernized, an airport was built with the aim of further developing Dubai's business potential. Dubai International Airport was opened by Sheikh Rashid in 1960. With an 1,800 metre runway, a small terminal building, control tower, firehouse, two duty-free shops and a parking lot for 500 vehicles, it bore little resemblance to today's busy and much larger hub, although the original terminal building still exists. Today some 105 airlines use the airport to connect to over 250 destinations worldwide.

From the start, an 'open-skies' policy was adopted. Any airline was allowed to use the airport without the restrictions or protectionist tactics that have proved so limiting to other international airports. This policy was originally intended to help Dubai become a major international hub, and, combined with seemingly constant improvements and expansion, it has proved immensely successful. The launch of Emirates airline and its growth in tandem with the airport and the economy of Dubai have also played a major part in the airport's development.

The size of the airport can be measured by its yearly passenger numbers. In 1980, it handled 2.8 million passengers; by 1990, that number had almost doubled to 5 million. In 2001, 13.5 million passengers used the airport; in 2002, the number increased to 16 million, 1 million more than forecast and an 18 percent increase on the previous year.[9] In 2010, 30 million passengers are expected, increasing to 45 million by 2030. Expansion works under way in early 2003 will create the capacity for around 60 million passengers when they are completed in 2006. The original two duty-free shops have grown into a major shopping experience, with a worldwide reputation among travellers. (See Appendix 6.)

Oil and Dubai

While the airport and Creek were being developed, the search for oil was in progress, as many of Dubai's neighbours had already struck it rich. Some of their wealth had trickled down to Dubai as they bought goods that were easily available there. In 1966, oil deposits were discovered offshore; and in 1969, oil revenues began to flow into Dubai. However, Dubai's oil reserves were known to be a mere fraction of those of neighbours such as Abu Dhabi and Saudi Arabia The government resolved to spend the oil money carefully, using it to fund a variety of major infrastructure projects. It is keen to reduce its dependence on oil, knowing that it may not last long into the 21st century. In 1990, oil accounted for 35 percent of GDP; by 2001, this had decreased to less than 10 percent. The aim is to reduce oil's share of GDP to just 1 percent by 2010, after which reserves are expected to be almost completely depleted.[10]

As Dubai was gearing up for oil production in the late 1960s, the UK announced its intention to withdraw from the area. This provided a fresh incentive for the ruling families of the Trucial States to discuss forming a federation. The rulers of Abu Dhabi and Dubai led the discussions, realizing that coming together as a federation would provide them with substantially increased political and economic stability, strengthening their position in the region.

In 1971 the British left and the United Arab Emirates came into being, made up of the emirates of Abu Dhabi, Dubai, Sharjah, Ajman, Umm Al Qaiwain and Fujairah. Ras Al Khaimah joined the following year.

The UAE is governed by a Federal Supreme Council consisting of the rulers of each of the seven emirates, with a president elected from within the group who serves for a five-year term. Each emirate has its own political and judicial powers, but foreign affairs, defence, healthcare and education are managed at the federal level.

Dubai is the second largest emirate after Abu Dhabi, which is also the capital of the UAE. Although Dubai enjoys the outward benefits of being part of the federation (such as in international relations and a shared defence strategy), it is seen by some to be in the shadow of the much richer Abu Dhabi. Moreover, in recent years Dubai appears to have struggled against some of the federal regulations, such as business ownership laws. Part of the reason for its creation of free zones was to overcome some of these restrictions.

Developing the infrastructure

The years following the discovery of oil and the formation of the UAE saw some of the most dramatic development of Dubai's infrastructure. Based on its traditional strengths in trade, the government built two ports and developed several heavy industries during the 1970s. These facilities have led to Dubai's position as one of the world's largest shipping centres.

A new port

In just a quarter of a century, the increases in trade have been dramatic. In 1975, imports were worth $1.93 million, exports $2.45 million and re-exports $1.52 million. By 2001, imports had increased to $22.7 billion, exports to $1.6 billion and re-exports to $6.2 billion.[11] In 2001, the main import sources were Japan, China, the US, the UK and India, and the main re-export destinations were Iran, India, Saudi Arabia, Kuwait and the US.[12] As an indication of the diversity and volume of this trade, Dubai has been among the world's leading exporters of wristwatches since the 1970s, despite the fact that not a single watch is manufactured in the UAE. (See Appendix 5.) Watches come from all corners of the globe and the majority go straight out again as re-exports.

The booming business in the Creek convinced the government that a larger deepwater harbour was needed to allow Dubai's growth as a port to continue. Much of the sea-going traffic then, as now, was in the form of dhows, traditional wooden cargo vessels used in the Gulf and neighbouring waters. With their distinctive raised bow and stern, and often seemingly overflowing with all manner of goods, these ships have changed little over the centuries. By 1966, around 4,000 dhows were arriving each year; larger ships were arriving too, but they had to anchor offshore and shuttle goods to the port on smaller boats.

Initial studies were based on four berths, but the design was modified during construction to include 16 berths. The port was completed in just five years and opened in 1972. Once again, the ambitious plans had been viewed by some with scepticism, but by the time the port opened there was a long line of ships waiting for berths. Early successes led to immediate expansion, and by 1978 a further 19 berths had been added.

Soon after the completion of the first phase of Port Rashid, the government announced its intention to develop an even larger port 35 kilometres from the centre of Dubai. At the time, there was spare capacity at the existing port, but the government believed that the new port would eventually be needed and it had a budgetary surplus with which to finance it.

In 1976, while the expansion of Port Rashid was under way, construction of Jebel Ali Port began with an initial investment of $2.5 billion (1976 prices). It opened only three years later. The first phase with 66 berths was completed in 1983, making it the largest man-made harbour in the world.

The management of Port Rashid and Jebel Ali was merged in 1991, and in the same year the combined ports handled 1 million TEUs (20-foot equivalent units, a standard measure used in shipping services) for the first time. In 2000, the ports were handling three times as much, and in 2002, they handled 4.2 million TEUs. The growth of port capacity continues, with a four-phase expansion project under way that is planned to increase it to 21.8 million TEUs by 2010.[13]

Heavy industries

As well as major infrastructure and ports, the government developed a series of heavy industries during the 1970s. With an initial investment of $1.4 billion (including share capital and long-term loans) in 1975, the Dubai Aluminium Company was established near Jebel Ali and is now one of the world's leading producers of aluminium and one of the world's most profitable smelters. Excess heat from the smelting process is used by a nearby desalination plant to produce around 25 million gallons of fresh water every day. Other industries hatched by the government during this time include a gas plant, dry dock and cable manufacturing plant.

Although these investments were intended to generate foreign currency revenue, they were also meant to send a signal to potential investors. As Mohammed Ali Alabbar, vice-chairman of Dubai Aluminium Company and Dubai Cable Company (in addition to being director general of the Department of Economic Development and chairman of Emaar Properties), explains:

Heavy industries are confidence-builders. Their development was a strategic move for Dubai, but it was also driven by solid investment criteria – it had to be commercially viable. At first, they may have underestimated the effect of building credibility; it's done much better than anyone expected.

Foreign investment and tourism

With the flow of trade continuing through Dubai's ports and airport, the government embarked on a series of projects that would continue throughout the late 1970s and 1980s, geared towards attracting foreign investment and further stimulating the economy.

The construction of the Dubai International Trade Centre was the first of these. When it was announced, it was viewed with reservation because it was to be located on the outskirts of the city (essentially in the desert) and there wasn't a perceived demand for a 39-storey office building at that time. But the project went ahead as planned and was completed in 1979. What would later become known as the World Trade Centre became home to a range of international businesses and consulates, as well as exhibition and conference facilities. It was also the first of many iconic building projects, with its distinctive silhouette visible for miles. Today, however, it is dwarfed by many taller towers in what is fast becoming Dubai's business and financial centre.

This period also saw the first wave of major hotels to be built in Dubai, with demand stimulated by the rapidly growing economy and resulting influx of visitors.

Today, for many people, Dubai may be synonymous with luxury hotels, but this is a recent development. The first purpose-built hotel was opened in 1959 with just eight rooms, later expanded to 35. Before then, business travellers had few options apart from staying in private homes; even Sheikh Rashid had an apartment on his property converted for guests. Other smaller hotels were built in the late 1960s, but the InterContinental was the first major chain hotel to be built in the city.[14]

Completed in 1975, the InterContinental was a haven for business travellers, and a shortage of alternative accommodation often led to people sleeping in the lobby or having to share double rooms. Other chains began building towards the end of the 1970s, but the Inter-Continental retains a place in Dubai's modern history that illustrates the dynamism and hustle-bustle of that time. Since then there has been huge growth in the hotel sector. In 2002, there were 272 hotels with 38,386 beds, compared with 42 hotels with 4,601 rooms in 1985.[15] Construction continues apace, with over 40 hotels planned for the first phase of the Palm Islands development. Some question whether so much additional hotel capacity is needed, but the government believes that visitor numbers will continue to increase and that there will be sufficient demand. (See Appendix 8.)

Another important part of the government's strategy to attract visitors has been Emirates airline. It provided $10 million as an initial investment to get the airline off the ground in 1985. Emirates is owned by the government of Dubai, but, like other government-owned companies, it operates independently without support or subsidy and has been profitable every year apart from its second in operation.

The airline is part of the Emirates Group, which also includes Dnata, a travel management services company. Group managing director Maurice Flanagan is careful to point out that Emirates has succeeded on its own merits, without any help or protection from the government. It remained profitable despite the travel industry downturn following the events of 11 September 2001, and during the Dubai Air Show in November 2001 the airline announced its intention to proceed with its order for $15 billion-worth of Airbus aircraft. At a time when many large airlines were cancelling aircraft orders and struggling to remain in business, this demonstrated Dubai's confidence in its ability to succeed.

As of the end of 2002, the airline served 62 destinations in 45 countries, and direct, non-stop flights to North America were planned to commence in 2003. Profits for the airline in the 2001–02 financial year amounted to $127.5 million, an increase of 11 percent on the previous year.[16] For the year ending March 2003, Emirates' profits were nearly double, at $246.9 million.[17] In 2003, as many of the world's largest airlines struggled, Emirates announced the largest aircraft order in civil aviation history, worth some $19 billion. The order included 21 Airbus A380-800 super-jumbos, bringing Emirates' current total order book to a value of around $26 billion.

The Jebel Ali Free Zone

Perhaps the most significant development of the 1980s was the Jebel Ali Free Zone, an industrial park that opened in 1985. The Jebel Ali Free Zone Authority, the regulatory agency for the area, offers attractive incentives for investors to locate in the zone. These include 100 percent foreign ownership, full repatriation of capital and profits, easy recruitment and sponsorship, and no currency restrictions. Outside the zone foreign businesses have to set up in partnership with a UAE national, who must own at least a 51 percent share of the business.

Jebel Ali Free Zone Authority also provides infrastructure for companies, ranging from basic services to fully built facilities, as well as local representatives to handle any administrative needs. As it is a free zone, there are no import or export duties on goods or equipment within the zone. It is located next to Jebel Ali Port, so investors have access to the port's facilities; however, the zone has attracted a wide range of businesses, not just those dependent on shipping. Initially, only subsidiary companies were allowed to operate in the zone, but after 1992 independent companies could be incorporated there. By the early 1990s, there were around 300 companies inside the zone; by 2003, the number had grown to 2,300 from over 100 countries.[18]

Apart from its intrinsic value to the economy of Dubai, the Jebel Ali Free Zone also set the stage for future developments, such as Dubai Internet City and Dubai Media City, which would apply similar models tailored to their own industries and workers.

The 1990s saw the development of a number of new industries in Dubai. The decade started with a new ruler as well. Following the death of Sheikh Rashid, his son, Sheikh Maktoum Bin Rashid Al Maktoum, became ruler, and five years later, he signed a decree appointing his brother, Sheikh Mohammed, Crown Prince. Sheikh Rashid had personally overseen the development of Dubai's significant infrastructure and industries since becoming ruler in 1958, and the involvement of his sons made them well-equipped to pick up where he left off.

New industries

While continuing to develop the infrastructure, the government turned its attention to new industries, particularly tourism, real estate and knowledge-based businesses.

Dubai set about developing its tourism sector in 1989 with the formation of the Commerce and Tourism Promotion Board, which has since become the Department of Tourism and Commerce Marketing. Initially, there were few attractions to lure tourists apart from the climate and the beaches. Although operating on a shoestring budget, the Department of Tourism and Commerce Marketing has been able to build the tourism trade through its work with tour operators and clever marketing.

Tourism is now the fastest-growing sector of Dubai's economy,[19] contributing about 12 percent to GDP in 2001.[20] Despite a global downturn in travel and tourism, the numbers continue to grow: about 3.6 million tourists visited Dubai in 2001[21] and about 4.5 million in 2002;[22] 15 million are expected in 2010.[23]

The development of luxury hotels and resorts has been crucial to the growth in tourism; the iconic Burj Al Arab, sometimes called the Eiffel Tower of the Middle East, has proved to be a major attraction in its own right.

Events and festivals have also been created to generate interest from abroad. Official sources estimate that the winter Dubai Shopping Festival attracted 1.6 million visitors in 1996, its first year, and

2.68 million visitors in 2002 who spent some $1.25 billion. In 2003, hotels were near full occupancy during the festival, with many rooms booked by residents of neighbouring states.[24]

The Dubai Summer Surprises festival was launched in 1998 to generate more tourism and shopping during the slow summer months, when temperatures can soar to the high 40s. This, too, has proven a major draw, with beaches filling up with intrepid European visitors. These festivals have also proven very popular with visitors from neighbouring countries.

Dubai has become a venue for many conferences and conventions, as well as for the Dubai Air Show and sporting events such as the Dubai World Cup horse race that draw visitors from around the world each year. These not only boost the local economy; they also provide valuable publicity, promoting Dubai's image around the world and throughout the region.

The next wave of development in Dubai came towards the end of the 1990s with Dubai Internet City and Dubai Media City. Sheikh Mohammed announced Dubai Internet City in October 1999 as a key part of his vision to attract the 'new economy' to Dubai. Taking advantage of the same type of free-zone status that had been so successful at Jebel Ali, the area was designed specifically to cater for the needs and desires of technology and media companies.

Research by Sheikh Mohammed's team had indicated that priorities for their target companies included full tax-free ownership, a solid technical infrastructure, and unfettered hiring and relocation of talent. Full ownership and no restrictions on hiring were easily built into the free-zone concept, but the infrastructure needed to be built, along with the buildings and landscaping. Sheikh Mohammed set a one-year deadline to complete the first phase of Dubai Internet City, which was to include not only designing and building the campus on what was then open desert, but also attracting and setting up businesses on the site.

Dubai Internet City was launched as planned in October of 2000 with full occupancy (85 companies) and a long waiting list.[25] As well as the technical infrastructure, the zone's management provides a 'one-stop shop' for all visas, licences and other support needs; it also organizes roadshows and exhibitions for its companies focusing on specific market segments.

By early 2003, among the 470 companies at Dubai Internet City were Microsoft, Oracle, Hewlett-Packard and IBM. The industry clustering seems to be working, too; one estimate suggests that more business is conducted among Dubai Internet City companies themselves than with outside clients.[26]

Dubai Media City was launched the following January, using the same model, concentrating on the needs of local, regional and international media businesses such as CNN, Reuters and Bertelsmann. Dubai Media City also attracted the headquarters or operational centres of various Pan-Arab media groups because of its openness. By the end of 2002, Dubai Media City was home to over 620 companies employing 3,000 workers and 170 freelances. The second phase of development has been completed, including further office space, shared service centres, retail outlets and restaurants, and construction of a third phase is under way.[27]

Dubai Media City will ultimately become home to more than just offices; projects currently under way include further commercial space, residential units and educational facilities. The residential units will be configured as open-plan lofts or villas with two, three or four bedrooms. These facilities are targeted at the growing workforce within Dubai Media City, but the development is open to all. This was just one of many residential and mixed-use projects being developed in early 2003.

The development also included the Dubai Ideas Oasis, a dotcom incubator that was put on hold after its first set of start-ups moved into Dubai Internet City or closed down. The Knowledge Village is another addition to the zone to be completed in 2003, offering electronic resources and facilities to attract e-learning, training and educational programmes, both home-grown and from abroad.

Residential and mixed-use facilities

In addition to the mushrooming business facilities that have appeared in Dubai in recent years, developers are also building residential and mixed-use facilities to support the growing population. Dubai Marina is a mix of high-rise and town-house units for some 40,000 people on the coast.

The Palm Islands is another development that attracted attention from around the world. The concept grew out of a need to expand Dubai's beaches for leisure use, and when complete it will add some 120 kilometres of coastline. It comprises two massive, man-made, palm-tree shaped islands extending into the Gulf, each protected by a crescent-shaped breakwater. Each Palm will have about 3,000 homes and 40 luxury hotels, plus complementary leisure and public facilities.

Following extensive feasibility studies, construction of the first Palm Island began in June 2001 and is expected to be open by early 2006, with the second opening about a year and a half later. The first Palm Island was designed as a 'retreat', with all available residential real estate selling within days; the second and larger Palm Island complex will be more of a tourism destination, with attractions including a water theme park, an aquarium and a 'Sea Village' themed area.

These are just a few examples. There are many more buildings going up in the centre of Dubai, stretching into the surrounding desert and into the sea. This is having a real impact on Dubai's economy: in 2000, real estate development represented about 9 percent of its GDP.[28]

Broadening the economic base

More recent initiatives aimed at broadening Dubai's economic base include two major projects – Dubai International Financial Centre and Dubai Silicon Oasis – which use the free-zone concept and are geared towards attracting new capabilities to the area.

Dubai International Financial Centre addresses the need for a stable, well-regulated financial centre in the area. In 2002, construction began on a 110-acre (44.6-hectare) site adjacent to the Emirates Towers complex just behind the gleaming high-rise office buildings lining Sheikh Zayed Road.

The financial centre model is based on the core values of 'integrity, transparency and simplicity', with the aim of creating a dynamic hub for institutional finance and a nexus for capital investment in the region. An important ingredient of the Dubai International Financial Centre is its regulatory framework. Recognizing this, the management has based its laws and regulations on best practices worldwide such as the UK's Financial Services and Markets Act of 2000. The financial centre hopes to attract $4 billion in revenue for its participants by 2006, which would double the contribution of financial services to Dubai's economy and will assist in developing the emirate's chances of becoming a major financial centre.[29]

The first phase of development includes The Gate, which will house the Dubai International Financial Centre's headquarters and first businesses. Subsequent phases will include leisure, education and residential facilities. The entire area will be linked with pedestrian walkways lined by parks, public spaces and retail arcades.[30]

Dubai Silicon Oasis was announced in the autumn of 2002, with construction planned to begin in 2003. The development will cover 6.5 million square metres in the Nad Al Sheba district. With the first phase planned for completion in 2006 or 2007, the zone's ambitious goal is to become 'the world's foremost centre of Silicon Intellectual Property creation and knowledge through high technology initiatives'. As the world's first purpose-built industrial park dedicated to the semiconductor industry, it is planned to house businesses from all parts of the semiconductor value chain and related industries, including semiconductor foundries, integrated device manufacturers, design and testing facilities, and research institutes.

While adding a high-value manufacturing industry to Dubai's portfolio, this project is also expected to provide educational opportunities for hundreds of UAE nationals over the first ten years through a combination of work experience and programmes at affiliated universities.[31] Although the semiconductor market may not have the appeal it once did, one major player is already interested: Communicant Semiconductor Technologies, a German firm, has committed to build a $1.7 billion plant within the area by 2007.[32]

In addition to these projects, an e-government portal was launched in the autumn of 2002 with 14 services for Dubai's residents, including payment mechanisms for various government fees and the ability to apply for licences and permits. By early 2003, over 150 transactional and more than 400 informational services were available via the portal. This service represents convenience for Dubai's residents, but it also reinforces the government's vision of Dubai as a modern, technologically advanced society. And crucially, it will for the first time provide real-time access to data.

Key themes

Dubai has achieved a lot in the past 40 years or so. Its location has helped: the emirate is ideally located to serve the growing markets in the Middle East, India, Pakistan, Iran and East Africa. It is also easy and relatively inexpensive, thanks to the free zones and an array of agencies and policies, for organizations to set up in and do business from Dubai. But there is much more to Dubai's success. Here is an overview of some of the key factors that have contributed to it.

Creating assets strategically

As Anis Al Jallaf, chairman of the Dubai International Financial Centre, says, Dubai was 'blessed with a lack of resources'. This view is shared among those who have known Dubai since the pre-oil days. The Earl of Home, chairman of Coutts, the UK's leading private bank, echoes this point, adding that Dubai 'couldn't just sit back and watch the money roll in – they had to learn other skills'.

People in Dubai were forced to think in new ways to create prosperity for themselves while their neighbours were cashing in on vast oil and gas reserves.

Dubai was forced to be smart from the start, building on its limited resources: a coastal location and a natural inlet. All infrastructural improvements and other developments had to be part of a vision that was grounded firmly in reality. Even when oil revenues began to flow into Dubai, the focus was on projects that would take it towards a diversified economy not dependent on oil.

Most of the emirate is desert. Building has been concentrated along the coast and around the Creek, stretching only a short way into the desert. But the government does not shrink from overcoming the apparent constraints on building; it is creating a new beachfront by building islands and cultivating vast oases of green living spaces in the middle of arid desert.

Vision and leadership is clearly important in deciding what should be done and ensuring that it gets done. Many in Dubai attribute much of the success of the emirate to the ruling Al Maktoum family. It's easy to see why, since they have been responsible for conceiving and driving major projects.

But it is not just about coming up with the projects and getting them done. It seems that every major project has a tale attached, describing how no one believed it could be done but the ruler knew better. Sheikh Rashid built and expanded the ports when few believed there was adequate demand. It was the same story with the World Trade Centre. More recently, Sheikh Mohammed indulged his passion for horses by setting up training stables in Dubai, defying established racing pundits in the US and the UK who claimed it couldn't be done. Godolphin Stables is now one of the largest and most successful stables in the world.

The government's willingness to accept risk is an important part of its ability to drive these projects. An early example of this is the modernization of the Creek, which was essentially financed by mortgaging Dubai itself.

Businesses have often proved more risk-averse than the government. On a number of occasions the government has invested in a new sector to get it established, with the aim of encouraging private investors to enter the market. The development of the luxury hotel sector is a good example. When a government-owned company, Jumeirah International, began to build some of the most distinctive and luxurious hotels in Dubai, it effectively raised standards and dared incumbents such as the InterContinental, Hyatt and Sheraton to try to keep up, attracting the attention of other leading hotel developers, almost all of which have since developed properties in Dubai.

Some examples of strategic asset creation include Port Rashid, the Jebel Ali Free Zone, Emirates airline, Dubai International Airport and the Palm Islands. The government undertook each of these at a crucial point in the development of the emirate, often despite daunting risk. Each one (with the exception of the Palm Islands, which are still under construction) has proved to be a valuable asset in Dubai's portfolio and, in parallel, has reinforced and added to the government's vision.

Accelerating growth

Growth in Dubai is not simply a matter of economic indicators; it is part of the culture. The notion of speed is pervasive, from racehorses to fast-track building construction. This is no coincidence. It is part of the Dubai model espoused by the rulers and another way that they lead by example. An often-repeated model in Dubai uses the example of a runner to explain how this works. It's important to keep running, and if you fall, you get right up again. But even if you do fall, because you're moving fast, you fall forward and get up ahead of where you were.

The acceleration effect has been created by bringing in the best from all over the world and putting them together: shipping companies in the ports and free zones; technology companies in Dubai Internet City; hoteliers in the red-hot tourism market; airlines at

Dubai International Airport. While many developing countries have adopted a protectionist approach, Dubai has done the opposite, stripping out restrictions and regulation to invite all comers. To ensure the most positive RSVPs, in many cases the government has researched exactly what would be most attractive to potential foreign investors then put those things in place. During the development of Dubai Internet City, for example, senior managers of the world's leading technology firms were asked what it would take to bring them to Dubai, and their answers were written into Dubai Internet City's blueprint, one of whom called it the client's 'wish list'.

As a result, both the business environment and the population of Dubai are tremendously diverse, with representation from dozens of countries and virtually every industry imaginable. The acceleration of value created by this variety of people and businesses only increases as further relationships are established across and within discrete industries.

Leadership also plays an important part, not just in creating free zones and courting foreign investment. Leaders in Dubai generally work within a framework of mutual trust, a legacy of its trading origins when a trader was taken at his word and there were no second chances. Trust between leaders and managers in both the public and private sectors often takes the place of formal rules or regulations, providing increased opportunity and freedom, and perhaps some temptation as well. Those who take advantage of this trust are dealt with severely, and unscrupulous traders get short shrift. But as Dubai continues to grow, maintaining this environment will be a challenge.

Leveraging key assets
In an open economy, the ability of leaders to step back and let growth take place can be as important as knowing when to intervene. This appears to be another strength of Dubai's rulers. They have created an environment that encourages investment and growth without stifling regulations or trade barriers.

This leverage can readily be seen in the hotel industry. The government accelerated growth by stimulating tourism and building a handful of landmark properties; then competitors from around the world quickly emerged to add their contributions to the mix. The same sort of leverage can be seen in Dubai Internet City and Dubai Media City, where a hospitable environment was created and growth has continued ever since. Or in the development of residential and mixed-used properties, which is rapidly transforming land from central Dubai to the barren desert nearby.

Further benefits of this leverage can be seen in the way that assets that have been created interact with and complement each other. The development of the airline, airport, hotels and tourist attractions is a good example of this.

Of course, this growth doesn't happen on its own. Although the government may step back to allow it to happen, it's part of a grand, articulated vision, the realization of which depends on trust. For example, Emirates is confident about investing billions in dozens of new super-jumbo jets because it trusts that tourist numbers will continue to rise, that the airport will have sufficient gates and hangars, and that there will enough hotel beds for the tourists to sleep in.

Managing the portfolio

Even though the government may step back and let growth happen, it takes care to remain in touch. Staying informed is crucial in managing growth and change.

Sheikh Mohammed is famously well-informed, as was his father, Sheikh Rashid. This was achieved through a combination of the *majlis* (the traditional forum in which leaders confer with their officials, hear grievances from the people and settle disputes) and personal involvement. Like his father, Sheikh Mohammed is a frequent visitor to the major projects he has instigated, checking progress and talking to managers and workers.

His senior officials, whom he meets regularly and at times daily, play an important role in keeping him in touch. Most of them have both governmental and business roles, which help ensure co-operation, while shared values and trust help prevent conflicts of interest. And Sheikh Mohammed also attends regular meetings with other leaders from Dubai's business community.

The accessibility of Dubai's rulers is strongly echoed in the management of government and business. The 'open-door' policy means that managers and even workers have the ear of someone who has the ear of Dubai Inc.'s CEO.

All this translates into a tight network of business and government leaders who work and communicate within a shared value structure towards common goals. This allows the government to judge when an asset needs investment to grow or to change in order to remain strategically useful, or when it is time to replace it with a different kind of asset that will contribute more to Dubai's economy.

Dubai has recently institutionalized various practices through the constitution of an Executive Council led by Sheikh Mohammed. Its members include heads of Dubai's government departments. This is meant to create greater co-operation between the departments. Plans are in the works to create localized councils through the recently announced Community Councils.

What next?

Many joke that there is no point in spending much time on business plans in Dubai because the actuals always overshoot the projections. This seems to have been the case from as far back as 1960, when the ruler repaid the Creek modernization loan much earlier than expected. But business planning is part and parcel of managing growth and Dubai has done its share.

In 2001 Sheikh Mohammed presented a comprehensive strategy for Dubai, setting out goals to achieve by 2010. These included becoming more integrated into the global economy; developing a knowledge economy; becoming known for innovation, dynamism and entrepreneurship; leveraging new and existing assets to create a powerful business network. A prominent part of the strategy involves making the most of Dubai's human resources by, for example, developing a new generation of young entrepreneurs; becoming a work environment of choice for talented knowledge workers; fully utilizing the female workforce; and taking advantage of the diversity of the population.[33] Such desire for broad and rapid growth is a characteristic that Sheikh Mohammed has been able to infect Dubai with. For example Anwar Gargash of Gargash Enterprises remembers one conversation with Sheikh Mohammed where he said his views on growth were, 'conquer, then conquer, then conquer'. This unending drive for change and success can be seen throughout Dubai today.

Stressing the importance of human resources and talent makes sense in light of the move towards a knowledge economy. It's also been an important factor in the growth of Silicon Valley and Singapore, with which comparisons are drawn in the following two chapters.

Notes

1 Government of Dubai, Department of Economic Development, *Development Statistics of Dubai 2002*; based on GDP figures for 2001, Table 2-1

2 Wilson, G. 1999. *Father of Dubai*. Dubai, UAE: Media Prima

3 Wilson, *Father of Dubai*

4 Department of Economic Development, *Development Statistics of Dubai 2002*

5 In 1997, the expatriate population was dominated by Indians and Pakistanis, representing 41 and 20 percent of the total respectively (MERAC/Edwards Economic Research Inc. GCC Demographic Report 1998 – from TEO)

6 The Executive Office, Dubai Data Series

7 Department of Economic Development, *Development Statistics of Dubai 2002*

8 Dubai 2010, from The Executive Office presentation

9 Dubai International Airport press release, from airport website

10 Dubai International Financial Centre, *An Economic Profile of Dubai*

11 The Executive Office, Dubai Data Series

12 Dubai International Financial Centre, *An Economic Profile of Dubai*, from Department of Economic Development, Socio-economic profile 2001

13 Dubai Ports Authority

14 Wilson, *Father of Dubai*

15 The Executive Office

16 Emirates Group Annual Report 2001–02

17 Emirates consolidated accounts for year ended 31 March 2003

18 Dubai Ports Authority

18 Dubai International Financial Centre, *An Economic Profile of Dubai*

20 *Gulf News*, 23 November 2002 (online)

21 Department of Tourism and Commerce Marketing

22 Interview with Khalid Bin Sulayem, director general, Department of Tourism and Commerce Marketing

23 Emirates Annual Report, 2002–03

24 Dubai Shopping Festival press release, 15 January 2003

25 From an interview with Ahmad Bin Byat, director general, Dubai Technology, Electronic Commerce and Media Free Zone

26 From an interview with Ahmad Bin Byat

27 Dubai Media City publicity

28 Dubai International Financial Centre, *An Economic Profile of Dubai*

29 Foggon, W., 'DIFC: Middle East meets West', *Emirates Investor*, 2 April 2002 (reprinted on Dubai International Financial Centre website)

30 www.gensler.com/masterplan

31 Preceding paragraphs: Dubai Silicon Oasis publicity

32 Reuters News, 12 October 2002

33 Dubai 2010, from The Executive Office presentation

3 Silicon Valley

Silicon Valley has been a refugee camp for revolutionaries who couldn't get a hearing elsewhere.

GARY HAMEL (from his book *Leading the Revolution*)

Silicon Valley is a region in northern California encompassing Santa Clara County and parts of several neighbouring counties with a population of more than 2 million. It is best known as the world's leading cluster of technology companies, including designers and manufacturers of the semiconductor, the chief ingredient of which gave the region its name. This chapter is included for three principal reasons.

First, Silicon Valley is a well-known model of organic growth. As such, it is useful to draw parallels and identify the organic elements in Dubai's growth model.

Second, there is general agreement about the 'ingredients' that led to the region's success. This set of ingredients can help us understand what has happened in Dubai. But it is not the ingredients alone that spell success. A great deal depends on the order in which they come together, how they are created if they don't already exist, and how they interact: in other words, the process.

Third, Silicon Valley is of interest in examining the success of Dubai because of its focus on technology and the value of intellectual capital. Dubai may be more easily compared to Singapore (see Chapter 4) because of their outward similarities, but each has based part of their growth strategies on a Silicon Valley model. Each has created technology districts to attract high-tech companies; each is seeking to stimulate entrepreneurship and innovation; and each has explicitly articulated an intention to move towards a knowledge economy. By first understanding how the Silicon Valley growth model worked, we will be in a better position to understand how Singapore and Dubai have leveraged parts of it.

A brief history

What has happened in Silicon Valley is remarkable. There are few corners of the world not touched by the technologies that grew from seeds planted there, and companies large and small have adopted management techniques that first took root in the region.

William Hewlett and David Packard would have had no idea of what was to come when they started Hewlett-Packard in 1939. With the encouragement of Professor Frederick Terman, the two Stanford graduates started a small business based on an electronic device Hewlett had developed while completing his masters thesis. Terman went so far as to lend them money personally as well as to help them get a loan from a local bank. The fledgling electronics firm operating from Packard's now-famous garage in Palo Alto had success with its early products, most famously with sales to Walt Disney, who used its oscillators during the production of *Fantasia*. But Hewlett-Packard's business really took off at the start of the Second World War, as the US government began ordering more and more of their electronic instruments.

There was more than enough government spending to go around at that time, and Sigurd and Russell Varian got their share. While also at Stanford, the two brothers developed a microwave receiver and transmitter called the klystron, which would prove to be an indispensable component of radar systems during the war. The Varians made a deal with the university that allowed them to use its physics lab and some materials in exchange for a 50 percent share of any resulting patents.[1] Not a bad deal for Stanford, which received almost $2 million as a result over the next 30 years.[2]

Hewlett-Packard, Varian Associates and other Silicon Valley firms grew substantially during the Second World War as a result of defence contracts, and the local economy grew with them. The US Department of Defense has been called 'the original "angel" of Silicon Valley'.[3] The largest employer in the region for years was Lockheed Missiles and Space (now Lockheed-Martin), at one point peaking at 28,000 workers in both manufacturing and R&D activities. Terman spent the war years on the faculty of Harvard, and when he returned to Stanford he had fresh insights. He had closely observed the symbiotic relationship between the north-eastern universities and neighbouring engineering firms, and he became committed to making the West Coast competitive, both commercially and intellectually.

Many of Terman's early initiatives are now considered prerequisites by would-be Silicon Valley imitators. He started by expanding the engineering department at Stanford with new faculty and programmes. To build relationships between students and local industry, the university organized field trips to businesses and events to inform managers about the latest research. Stanford established a research lab dedicated to practical applications. This was considered somewhat heretical at the time, but was important for forming links with businesses. An executive education programme was set up for local engineers, bringing them and their ideas into a stimulating, collaborative academic environment. The Stanford Research Park was set up on nearby land owned by the university. Varian Associates moved their offices to the Research Park and others quickly followed, attracted largely by its close proximity to the campus. These programmes were crucial in the early development of the professional and social infrastructure of the area, providing great opportunities for those in industry and the university to mingle and co-operate.

An ambition to compete with the East Coast wasn't all Terman brought back from Harvard. He also brought a wealth of business and government contacts, which he quickly put to use, courting investment in research and industry in the Valley.

Although many contend that the genesis of Silicon Valley was the founding of Hewlett-Packard in 1939 (and some even believe it was much earlier), others believe that the formation of Shockley Transistor Corporation in 1954 was the critical event in the region's history. But whichever view you subscribe to, the real action started in 1956 when eight of Shockley Transistor's senior managers left to start a competing venture backed by New York's Fairchild Camera and Instrument Corporation.

Fairchild Semiconductor started well, selling its first 100 transistors to IBM for $150 each.[4] But it wasn't until Robert Noyce at Fairchild invented the integrated circuit[5] that sales really took off. The patent was awarded in 1961, and two years later sales had reached $130 million, largely as a result of government contracts.

Myriad start-up companies were hatched by Fairchild alumni, including Advanced Micro Devices Inc., National Semiconductor Corporation, and Intel Corporation. Along with an entrepreneurial spirit and technical know-how, those who jumped ship from Fairchild brought with them a casual, laid-back management style that would come to typify Silicon Valley companies and would later spread to many other businesses in the US and other parts of the world.

Others left Fairchild (and other tech firms) to become venture capitalists, reinvesting their new-found fortunes in the growing technology industry in the area. Even Stanford got into the act, investing a portion of its endowment in new ventures in the region. The new venture capitalists brought with them more than bulging wallets; because many of them were highly experienced engineers with local business experience, they brought a bulging Rolodex with contacts and referrals, and they could also provide first-hand advice.

As the prosperity of the region grew, a new business and social culture grew around it. Companies were less formal and less hierarchical. People began to place more value on social and professional networks than on the organizations they were working for. Changing jobs frequently was accepted and even encouraged, reinforcing and accelerating the spread of the emerging value system. This led to information and ideas sharing among individuals within their networks, something that had rarely happened before.

The proliferation of start-ups wasn't limited to semiconductor companies. The need for supporting businesses and other links in the semiconductor value chain brought to the Valley a range of new businesses such as law firms, headhunters and specialized testing and design operations.

The comfortable position of the Silicon Valley chipmakers came under threat in the 1980s from Japanese firms, which were producing higher-quality chips at lower cost. Many of the established players panicked and switched course in an attempt to beat the Japanese at their own game of mass production.

The large Silicon Valley firms struggled, and many of their best engineers left to create a new wave of start-ups, involved in the design and production of semi-custom and speciality chips. The result was that mass-manufacture of memory chips shifted to Asia, while research and development and more specialized, higher-margin manufacture remained in the Valley.[6]

The new ventures that emerged in the 1980s were able to build on the strengths of the existing network of suppliers and infrastructure and the pool of talent. With the backing of venture capitalists, they were able to build businesses that produced a broader mix of tech products.

Firms generally avoided vertical integration, preferring to specialize within the complex value web that was emerging. Established in 1982, Sun Microsystems is an example of the new generation of Silicon Valley start-ups which made an early decision to concentrate on their core competencies and relied on trusted suppliers for all else, while still managing the overall process. Because of this approach, firms like Sun Microsystems are able to respond to changing technologies, market conditions and customer demands quickly while still sharing risk with their partners.[7]

An organic recipe

The success of Silicon Valley is founded on several ingredients: universities and research institutes, a sophisticated service infrastructure, available knowledge workers, customers, lead users and early adopters.[8]

Universities and R&D

Before Hewlett, Packard or the Varian brothers arrived, there was Stanford University, which was founded in 1885. It seems clear that the initial seeds came from Stanford, and it was Frederick Terman who took the initiative to scatter them in the Valley. AnnaLee Saxenian describes him as a 'social and institutional innovator' and credits him with shaping 'the relationships among individuals, firms, and institutions in Silicon Valley, creating a community that has encouraged continuous experimentation and technological advance'.[9]

Terman saw the importance of exposing his researchers to the business world, as well as bringing the business world into the university to create the kind of synergistic, co-operative environment that he knew would spell success for the region.

But it wasn't just Stanford that educated the minds of those in the Valley. Programmes at the University of California, Berkeley, as well as local community colleges soon emerged to complement Stanford's contribution. As a result of the success of the co-operation between the academic and business worlds, there soon appeared R&D facilities of some of the most well-known technical innovators: Lockheed Aerospace, Westinghouse, ITT, IBM and Xerox's Palo Alto Research Center (PARC).

Of course, there's no way of knowing what might have happened in Silicon Valley without Terman's leadership and support. The region was already home to a number of radio technology companies[10] when Stanford started to spin out its first tech start-ups. But there is no doubt that the university was an early attraction for the skilled knowledge workers who started the growth of the network, and it seems likely that without the support of Terman, people like Hewlett, Packard and the Varian brothers would have ended up working for established companies in the east of the US.

Skilled knowledge workers

It's clear that the highly skilled engineers being educated by Stanford were a crucial part of the early successes of Silicon Valley. As the number of tech businesses grew and Stanford's programmes expanded, workers in the region became nodes in the network that was being created. As they moved between industry and academia, and from company to company, their personal contacts and the depth and breadth of their knowledge became more extensive.

This also helped to spread the emerging culture that would become typical of the region. Hewlett-Packard, one of the first and most enduring success stories, established a working culture distinct from the formal, hierarchical environment associated with most organizations at the time, particularly at engineering firms in the east. 'The HP Way' was the nickname for this way of working, and it quickly became characteristic of the rebellious attitude shared by Silicon Valley workers.[11] The frequency of job changes and managers leaving to start new ventures helped to spread this culture across the Valley, and the mobility of workers led to cross-pollination of ideas and knowledge from firm to firm.

In Silicon Valley, therefore, success was not solely due to the ready availability of knowledge workers; the role of the network and its primary nodes as carriers of a shared culture and technical knowledge added another important dimension.

Early adopters

None of the Silicon Valley start-ups would have got far without early adopters who were all too willing to buy new and unproven products. In Silicon Valley, the US military filled this role, and it continues to do so (though to a lesser extent) today. Walt Disney Studios may have been Hewlett-Packard's first major customer, but it was military contracts that fuelled much of HP's subsequent growth.

In an essay in *Understanding Silicon Valley*, Stewart W. Leslie, a Johns Hopkins University professor, points out that the role of defence spending is often overlooked in the analysis of Silicon Valley successes.[12] He reasons that failure to find a substitute for such early adopters can lead to the demise of would-be imitators. This rings true, particularly considering that this spending often went to initial orders for complex technical products while they were still on the drawing board, which amounts to an R&D grant combined with a substantial guaranteed production order.[13]

While companies such as Hewlett-Packard found markets in addition to defence and aerospace, others such as Varian Associates and Litton depended on large government contracts thanks to their expertise with microwave tubes, guidance systems and complementary technologies. Such contracts proved crucial for their growth and demonstrated great faith in the abilities of the Silicon Valley firms because, at that time, to make a substantial investment in small, young ventures was regarded as extremely risky.[14]

It seems clear that without its share of the military spending spurred by the Second World War, the Korean War, the Space Race and the Cold War, Silicon Valley would probably never have got off the ground as a technology cluster.

Service infrastructure

Another important element in the development of Silicon Valley was the robust service infrastructure. Martin Kenney, a professor at the University of California, Davis, and Urs Von Burg, a PhD candidate at the University of St Gallen in Switzerland, call it 'Economy

Two', the network of supporting service organizations that enable 'Economy One' to prosper. In their model, Economy One consists of the established tech firms and research institutions.

Just as front-office operations need the back-office to work, Economy Two allows Economy One to exist and, more importantly, to reproduce.[15] In this model, the service infrastructure consists of an interconnected network of firms such as law firms, investment banks, recruitment agencies, marketing agencies, accountancy firms and other highly specialized service providers.

Importantly, the firms that make up this group have the local industry experience and knowledge of the network and available resources that allow them to go beyond their normal role. Legal firms in particular serve a function beyond what their letterheads may indicate; they are frequently dealmakers and counsellors, or a combination of these, and may also undertake 'matchmaking' or help to arrange financing.[16]

A primary role of these firms is to serve start-ups. Although a top-tier branding agency might still work with well-known brands, firms within the network have the experience and tentacles in the network to enable them to advise and get the start-up company moving. The need for this local knowledge and network presence prompted many New York investment banks to set up local offices because they were unable to serve this market from the other side of the country.

Planners attempting to recreate the Silicon Valley model ignore the service infrastructure at their peril, because the unique needs of start-ups and, later on, focused industry clusters depend on the support that this infrastructure provides. Furthermore, Kenney and Von Burg point out that the strength of Economy Two in Silicon Valley was reinforced by the continual successes of industry feeding the growth and sophistication of the supporting businesses. This implies a high degree of co-dependence between start-up businesses and the service infrastructure, which becomes increasingly effective as growth continues. The risk for would-be

Silicon Valley imitators is that supporting businesses cannot hope to be optimally effective without time to learn and develop based on the needs of the industry they hope to underpin.

Available venture capital

By 1974 there were more than 150 venture capital firms in Silicon Valley, and Stanford was also using part of its endowment to provide venture capital.[17] It is an interesting fact that much of the venture capital in the Valley was home-grown.

The success of Fairchild Semiconductor and its progeny created tremendous wealth for their founders and employees, and much of this wealth was reinvested in start-ups via venture capital funds. Because Valley venture capitalists, such as Eugene Kleiner and Floyd Kvamme of Kleiner Perkins, and Donald Valentine and Pierre Lamond of Sequoia Partners, were already integral players in the network with a wealth of technical knowledge, they were invariably able to provide advice and contacts as well as funding.

In their essay in *Understanding Silicon Valley*, Martin Kenney and Richard Florida make the important point that the venture capital system grew up along with the Valley as an integral part of the network, serving to fuel and attract new ventures while adding further robustness to the fabric of the business environment.[18] The co-dependent, mutually reinforcing nature of this relationship is similar to the one between the Economy One and Economy Two companies discussed earlier, further illustrating the complexity and robustness of the Silicon Valley ecosystem.

Complementary organizations

The final component that makes Silicon Valley work is the presence of complementary organizations, or 'production networks', as Saxenian calls them.[19] Not to be confused with the service infrastructure discussed above, these organizations work together to create a value-added product as links in a value chain or nodes in a value web.

Many of the new wave of tech start-ups that emerged in the Valley in the 1980s grasped this concept immediately. Sun Microsystems is a good example.[20] The computer workstation company specialized in designing, testing and prototyping hardware and software, but it left manufacture to a vast network of suppliers. This not only ensured that Sun's overheads were kept low, but it also enabled it to react faster, reduce risk and stay on top of the latest manufacturing technologies. Production networks like this, when managed well, also create lots of opportunities to share learning and accelerate innovation. It's important to note, however, that this model works best in fast-moving, volatile markets, when innovation is an important factor.

Lessons from the Valley

If assembling the ingredients discussed above was all there was to it, there would be Silicon Valleys springing up all over the world. But there have been enough attempts to recreate the phenomenon to confirm that it's not that simple. As David Rosenberg shows in *Cloning Silicon Valley*, even the top six would-be tech hubs – Cambridge (UK), Helsinki (Finland), Tel Aviv (Israel), Bangalore (India), Singapore and Hsinchu-Taipai (Taiwan) – all leave something to be desired.[21]

What are they doing wrong? In many cases, imitators fail to recognize that Silicon Valley was an organic process. Even if all the ingredients can be assembled for a new tech region, the personal and industrial networks in Silicon Valley developed a robustness over time that would be hard to replicate.

Looking back at the Silicon Valley story, we can see how the organic growth occurred and the path dependencies inherent in the process. The university and its research centre came first, and further research and skilled engineers soon followed. The initial tech firms grew quickly as a result of the spending of the military, a prominent early adopter. Then the service infrastructure grew to support the developing industry, often run by alumni of older, established firms. Venture capital and complementary organizations also emerged, largely thanks to the wealth generated by existing firms and the demands of the diversifying range of interrelated industries. The networks created in the process enabled the industry to weather the shake-out of the 1980s, forming a new generation of tech firms; although the jury's still out on how the region will weather the downturn that has followed the bursting of the dotcom bubble.

It is interesting to consider, then, how rapid growth can be achieved without an organic process, or even all the elements looked at above. Is there a way to create the missing elements and make it work? The answer depends on contextual factors, such as culture, the business environment, prevailing public policy and any number of other variables. In Silicon Valley, these contextual factors combined in a way that helped it to be successful.

Corporate culture

The corporate culture that thrived in Silicon Valley was less formal, more collaborative and less hierarchical than was the norm in traditional firms outside the region. This culture grew out of a shared 'outsider' mentality that separated the region from its established competitors on the East Coast, and it was defined and communicated by managers at Hewlett-Packard and Fairchild.

On a higher level, this was happening within the broader American – or, more specifically, northern Californian – culture that values individual achievement and encourages entrepreneurs. This should be an important consideration for those applying this model elsewhere, especially within national cultures that tend to be risk-averse.

Business environment

The business environment is another important contextual factor. The growth of Silicon Valley began when demand for the technologies it was churning out was starting to explode. The Valley's industry has, on the whole, also been able to adapt its offerings to address changes in the market over the years.

The technology industry is characterized by rapid change and rampant innovation, and the network model works well precisely because it is able to accommodate the web of interrelated organizations and their partners and suppliers. As the large chipmakers discovered in the 1980s when the rug was pulled from under them, the Silicon Valley model supports specialization and discourages vertical integration.

Public policy

Public policymakers have a role to play as well. By determining the regulatory, tax, infrastructure and zoning policies, officials can make the difference between a stifling, inhospitable place to do business and an easy, welcoming one.

Silicon Valley benefited directly from favourable tax treatment and indirectly through the relaxation of laws governing venture capital.[22] Public policy can also help take some of the sting out of the negative side of growing prosperity in a region, including traffic congestion, housing price inflation and pollution.[23]

What next?

The collapse of technology (and many other) stocks at the start of the 21st century put a new spin on the Silicon Valley model as an exemplar for rapid growth. Past successes are now part of history and much of the Valley has lost confidence and is in disarray.

At the end of 2002, Deloitte & Touche's Silicon Valley Venture Capital Confidence Survey was full of gloomy predictions: in 2003 there would be more private company failures than ever, venture capitalists would shy away from the unfamiliar, small companies would be bought up by larger ones, and so on. The chaos currently prevailing in the Valley makes it difficult to draw any specific conclusions, but it may be worth noting that the organic growth of the region will inevitably leave it exposed to external factors.

Nevertheless, the tough times in the Valley don't seem to be discouraging others from seeking inspiration from its happier days. If all goes to plan, Dubai's Silicon Oasis will soon be following in Silicon Valley's footsteps. The question that remains is whether the emirate will be able to assemble the right ingredients using an appropriate process as it makes the transition to a knowledge economy.

Notes

1 Saxenian, A. 1994. *Regional Advantage: Culture and Competition in Silicon Valley and Route 128.* Cambridge, Massachusetts: Harvard University Press

2 Saxenian's footnote 26 on p. 21, referring to a paper by Edward Ginzton in *IEEE Spectrum*, February 1975

3 Leslie, S. W. 2000. 'The Biggest "Angel" of Them All: The Military and the Making of Silicon Valley'. In *Understanding Silicon Valley*, ed. M. Kenney, p. 49. Stanford, California: Stanford University Press

4 From www.pbs.org

5 Jack Kilby of Texas Instruments is acknowledged to have developed the IC at the same time, but the patent was awarded to Fairchild first; www.pbs.org

6 Preceding history based on Saxenian, pp. 84–95

7 Saxenian, A. 'Origins and Dynamics of Networks'. In *Understanding Silicon Valley*

8 Bahrami, H. & Evans, S. 'Flexible Recycling and High-Technology Entrepreneurship'. In *Understanding Silicon Valley*, p. 166

9 Saxenian, A. 1995. 'Creating a Twentieth Century Technical Community: Frederick Terman's Silicon Valley'. Paper prepared for inaugural symposium on 'The Inventor and the Innovative Society', The Lemelson Center for the Study of Invention and Innovation, National Museum of American History, Smithsonian Institution, 10–11 November 1995

10 Sturgeon, T. J. 'How Silicon Valley Came to Be'. In *Understanding Silicon Valley*

11 Saxenian, *Regional Advantage*, cited by Leslie in *Understanding Silicon Valley*

12 Leslie in *Understanding Silicon Valley*, p. 49

13 Leslie in *Understanding Silicon Valley*, p. 50

14 Leslie in *Understanding Silicon Valley*, p. 50

15 Kenney, M. & Von Burg, U. in *Understanding Silicon Valley*

16 Suchman, M. C. 'Dealmakers and Counselors: Law Firms as Intermediaries in the Development of Silicon Valley'. In *Understanding Silicon Valley*, p. 79

17 *Understanding Silicon Valley*, p. 211

18 Kenney, M. & Florida, R. 'Venture Capital in Silicon Valley: Fueling New Firm Formation'. In *Understanding Silicon Valley*

19 Saxenian, *Regional Advantage*, pp. 145–6

20 Saxenian, *Regional Advantage*, p. 141

21 Rosenberg, D. 2002. *Cloning Silicon Valley*. London: Pearson Education

22 Kenney & Florida in *Understanding Silicon Valley*, p. 114

23 Saxenian, *Regional Advantage*, pp. 167–8

4 Singapore

For a country to rise from the threshold of subsistence to one of the highest living standards in the world in 30 years is no common achievement.

JACQUES CHIRAC, commenting on Singapore

If Silicon Valley has achieved its growth organically, bottom up, Singapore has grown in the opposite way: top down. Silicon Valley was left to market forces, whereas the leaders of Singapore since its independence have calculatedly driven the country forward to achieve its growth.

A brief history

Newly independent in 1965 after a brief two years as part of Malaysia and over 100 years under British rule, Singapore's government had its work cut out. The country had to gain international recognition, secure its borders and build an economy. With no natural resources, a minuscule domestic market, reluctant neighbouring trading partners and high unemployment, Lee Kuan Yew, the prime minister, made a commitment to transform Singapore into a dynamic, prosperous independent country. It was an ambitious goal for a largely undeveloped country of 2 million squeezed on to an island of only 250 square miles. Lee and his staff sought advice wherever they could find it, on industrial development, defence and tourism.

Early efforts to kick-start the economy included promoting

tourism abroad and encouraging new factories and small businesses. But despite such moves unemployment continued to rise. It was the loss of the British military presence in 1971 (the same year the British pulled out of Dubai) that provided the spur for Singapore's transformation to begin. The British military had accounted for 20 percent of Singapore's GDP, occupied 11 percent of the total landmass and employed 30,000 people. An aggressive development programme meant that by the end of 1971 all the real estate that the British had used had been reallocated, much of it for use by foreign investors, transport or leisure facilities.

Lee Kuan Yew's government decided that the key to Singapore's growth would be multinational companies. The Economic Development Board set about attracting them to the country by providing better trading conditions than its neighbours and raising its standards to those of the West. The government paved the way by building solid infrastructure and transport systems, providing fiscal incentives, promoting exports and building industrial parks. By the mid-1970s, Texas Instruments, National Semiconductor, Hewlett-Packard and General Electric had all set up in Singapore.

At first the local workforce was enthusiastic but lacked skills, so public and private training schemes were put in place. Courses for factory workers were set up in conjunction with investors and local government. These produced skilled technicians and unemployment was soon reduced to a tiny percentage of the workforce.

As well as becoming a home away from home for foreign multinationals, Singapore set out to become a financial centre. The first steps were taken in the late 1960s, when one of Lee Kuan Yew's advisers noted that Singapore could fit neatly in the gap between markets closing in San Francisco and opening in Zurich. The government attracted foreign financial institutions by removing taxes on interest earned by non-residents. By starting slowly and creating an international reputation for integrity in financial markets, Singapore had developed into a leading banking centre by the 1990s.

Singapore was already an important port by the time it became independent. In 1819 Sir Thomas Stamford Raffles, an Englishman, had signed a treaty with the sultan of neighbouring Jahore, establishing Singapore as a trading station for the East India Company. Shortly thereafter, it was declared a free port. As a major stopover point on the route between the Indian Ocean and the South China Sea, the port flourished and developed during the 19th and 20th centuries. Today, Singapore is one of the busiest ports in the world, handling 16.8 million TEUs (twenty-foot equivalent units) in 2002, with 250 shipping lines sailing to 600 ports worldwide.[1]

As part of the quest to raise standards in Singapore, Lee Kuan Yew set in motion a huge range of improvement projects. Strict 'clean and green' measures were adopted, ranging from comprehensive landscaping and planting programmes to prohibition of the sale of chewing gum, smoking and spitting in public. Strict anti-pollution and traffic-calming measures were also put into place.

When Changi airport was redeveloped and reopened in 1981, it was the largest airport in Asia. Together with Singapore Airlines, it has made Singapore even more accessible, as well as boosting its international reputation. By developing their ports, airports and airlines, both Dubai and Singapore were able to build on their existing strengths as entrepôts and their strategic locations to accelerate their development as international business centres.

English is the working language in Singapore and one of four official languages in schools. This policy was contentious when it was introduced – many faculty members spoke no English at the time – but it has borne fruit. Widespread fluency in English has helped create a hospitable environment for foreign companies locating in Singapore. It has also provided a common secondary language for Malay, Mandarin and Tamil speakers and helped Singaporeans learn to find their way around the internet efficiently.

Lee Kuan Yew's paternalistic policies created stability, prosperity and order for his people, although sometimes at the expense of individual freedoms, particularly among the media and political dissenters. He stepped down in 1990, appointing his trusted deputy to take his place, but Lee Kuan Yew remains a 'senior minister' and is an active force in the government.

When Lee Kuan Yew took office in 1959, GDP per head was $400.[2] When he stepped down, it was $12,200.[3] By 2001 it had reached $20,880, ranking Singapore as one of the 20 richest countries in the world.

But Singapore may have become a victim of its own success. After decades of prosperity, the government began to doubt that growth could continue based on its core industries (petroleum refining, petrochemicals, electronics assembly, and trade-related and financial services[4]). So in 1997 the government began working towards a transition to a knowledge-based economy, creating programmes designed to foster entrepreneurship and innovation, putting in place a range of supporting services. This appears to be presenting a substantial challenge. The Global Entrepreneurship Monitor study, which evaluated the entrepreneurial activity of 21 countries in 2000, ranked Singapore near the bottom, ahead of only Japan and Ireland.[5] The study found that only 2.1 percent of adults aged 18–64 were currently setting up or running a new business; in the US, the corresponding figure was found to be 12.7 percent.

Putting it together

The challenge for Singapore was quite different from that faced by Silicon Valley. For Singapore it was a matter of survival, not just competitiveness, and Lee Kuan Yew concluded that:

> An island city-state in South-east Asia could not be ordinary if it was to survive. We had to make extraordinary efforts to become a tightly knit, rugged, and adaptable people who could do things better and cheaper than our neighbours, because they wanted to bypass us and render obsolete our role as entrepôt and middleman for the trade of the region. We had to be different.[6]

Creating the ingredients

The previous chapter outlined the principal components or ingredients that contributed to the success of Silicon Valley. Since Singapore had none of these in place when Lee Kuan Yew took office, they had to be created. If the country was to attract US multinationals, it would have to provide both the infrastructure and the levels of service these investors would demand.

The Economic Development Board (EDB) was established in 1961 before independence to help put the economy on a stronger footing in anticipation of the British withdrawal, and specifically to woo foreign investment primarily in four industries: ship breaking and repair, metal engineering, chemicals, and electrical equipment and appliances.[7] As a statutory board, it had a degree of independence while remaining ultimately under government control. Its role was to do whatever might be necessary to get foreign investors to close the deal. This included finding land and facilities, hiring and training staff, providing any required infrastructure, providing attractive fiscal incentives and tax relief (or direct investment in some cases) and generally helping to overcome any difficulties.[8]

Like Silicon Valley, Singapore needed the key ingredients of higher education and R&D, skilled knowledge workers, early adopters, supporting industry and services, venture capital and complementary organizations. But its starting point necessitated a completely different approach. Thus the EDB began courting foreign investment at the same time as building infrastructure to suit investors' current and future needs.

An often-told example from the 1970s shows how the EDB worked. Singapore was chosen from a shortlist of four countries for a manufacturing plant for Hewlett-Packard. Representatives of the EDB impressed HP with their enthusiasm, willingness, energy and ability to articulate what HP could expect. In essence, the EDB provided a 'one-stop shop' for HP throughout the process. The degree to which the EDB would extend itself was illustrated once the deal was done and William Packard planned to make a site visit. The electrical systems needed to power the elevator to the sixth-floor facility were not in place by the date of his visit. So a representative of the Jurong Town Corporation (a spin-off of the EDB that managed land development and buildings) decided to power the new HP facility's lights and elevator with an immense cable strung from a nearby building.[9]

The EDB was selective about the types of industry it would court. It was interested only in attracting multinationals that would bring long-term investment and growth, technologies that would complement Singapore's growing portfolio of industries and opportunities for skilled employment. HP fitted the bill, and the firm enthusiastically entered into a co-operative relationship with Singapore.

In parallel to the EDB's activities in encouraging foreign investment, a wide variety of infrastructure projects have been undertaken since the early 1960s. One of the earliest, and largest, was the Jurong industrial estate. It was considered a risky venture at the time, being built speculatively on reclaimed swampland on the western side of the island. Spun out of the EDB in the late 1960s, the Jurong Town Corporation develops and manages properties including industrial estates, business parks, science parks and other specialized industrial zones, many developed speculatively.

Further important infrastructure improvements included continuing development of the seaport, building the new airport and improvement of the road network. More recent projects have been geared towards building the information technology infrastructure. Singapore ONE is a government programme encompassing the development of a high-bandwidth infrastructure that will make broadband internet access available to all Singaporeans and the development of applications and services that take advantage of this network. Infocomm 21 is Singapore's strategic plan for developing its 'infocomm' industry and allowing all aspects of the public and private sectors to make the most of these technologies.

Skilled knowledge workers

When Singapore became independent, it was often said that its only resource was its people. Although initially divided by language, culture and religion, Singaporeans were hard working and willing to learn.

Increasing the supply of talent proved a challenge. Beginning in the early 1970s, the government granted scholarships to outstanding cadets in the military in exchange for an eight-year commitment to the service. A similar programme was put in place to groom top scholars. Many of them went on to attend graduate school at a leading Western university before returning to Singapore to take a post in the civil service, on a statutory board, or in a government-linked company. This scheme demonstrated the willingness of the government to learn from outside sources. Programmes with a wider scope were established in the early 1980s to address the loss of highly skilled Singaporeans who were emigrating. Adopting a model similar to the EDB's, outposts were set up in various countries to recruit well-educated people.[10]

On a larger scale, incoming multinationals and government training schemes have created a rich pool of talent that helps attract foreign investors. In the early days, the EDB often conducted week-long training sessions to teach inexperienced workers the basics of factory work, including the importance of discipline and turning up on time.[11] More advanced technical training was made available as demands on the labour market increased. In many cases, incoming multinationals provided training programmes as well, frequently in conjunction with the EDB, as part of an incentive package. And some foreign governments set up and financed training centres in Singapore to provide technical skills for local workers.[12]

In 1979, the government launched the Skills Development Fund to help employers provide training for their least-skilled workers. The scheme imposed a levy on employers with low-paid workers, then used the funds to share the cost of training with participants.

The catch is that eligible training programmes must be 'relevant to the economic development of Singapore'. This is a good example of how the Singapore government has been able to share with the private sector the costs and responsibility of broadening and deepening the indigenous skills base. The scheme seems to have been a success, having supported about 8 million training places since its inception.[13]

As on-the-job learning increased, the collective experience of the workforce in areas such as electronics had become a major asset for Singapore. It was one of the main reasons firms such as Seagate were attracted to the country, thus laying the foundations for a hard disc drive technology cluster in Singapore.[14]

In the past decade, more programmes have been put in place to attract foreign talent and entrepreneurs to Singapore. In keeping with the government's stated objectives of moving the country away from manufacturing to knowledge-based industry, the education system is being revamped to encourage more creativity and entrepreneurship. This is precisely what is required, according to the Global Entrepreneurship Monitor study, which indicates that schools have not focused enough on encouraging such qualities. This may be because the ingrained collective culture has not encouraged individualism or risk, and because the government has tended to encourage brighter students to pursue engineering and technical studies exclusively, instead of the humanities and arts, which it now realizes are important to stimulate the creative thinking it is seeking to foster. The study also shows that the most popular career choices are with large, established companies, not start-ups. Another finding indicates that people under 35 and those with higher education (especially at the tertiary level) are most likely to engage in entrepreneurial activities.

Universities and R&D
Singapore's universities have traditionally been good at churning out graduates with specific skills, but not so good at encouraging

innovation and creativity. Curricula at universities and polytech-
nics are being overhauled to stimulate creative thinking, and inter-
disciplinary programmes are being offered involving interaction
between Singaporean and overseas students.

The Ministry of Education allocated funds in 2002 to create a
new polytechnic and maybe another university, and the addition of
programmes in 'creative reasoning and other skills essential for
the knowledge-based economy'. Adult education is also being
upgraded.[15]

The government began a campaign to develop more research
and development activity in Singapore in 1991 with the formation
of the National Science and Technology Board, which became the
Agency for Science, Technology and Research (A*STAR) in 2002.
A*STAR is an umbrella organization for councils focusing on biomedical research and science and engineering. It also has an
agency that manages intellectual property and a division that
helps with administrative support. At the end of 2000, the state
accounted for 37 percent of R&D spending in Singapore, and
efforts are under way to encourage more private-sector spending.
Since the late 1990s, the EDB has been responsible for providing
R&D assistance to the private sector and has various grants and
incentives at its disposal.

The Singapore Science Parks were established in 1980 to serve as
a focal point for R&D in the region. By 2000, over 300 businesses
were established on the site, almost half focusing on information
technology. One North is a new development that will include
space for offices and business services, biomedical research facilities, an entertainment and media complex, hospitality and conference facilities, and an incubator for 'technopreneurs'. Phase Z.Ro,
the incubator, had about 50 tenants at the end of 2002.

These initiatives are geared towards increasing local R&D;
multinationals account for most of the current private-sector
R&D investment.[16] In a 1999 paper by Hang Chang Chieh, the
author suggests that in order to create a sustainable indigenous

R&D culture in Singapore the role of a research engineer must represent a respectable career and the path to commercialization of innovations must be well-marked.[17] If this is the case, it follows that the future success of R&D in Singapore will depend on the success of the efforts to create a culture that nurtures entrepreneurs and innovators.

Available venture capital

Prominent international venture capitalists operate in Singapore, but the government also has a major role in providing venture capital to budding entrepreneurs. Cumulatively, the venture capital industry in Singapore had raised $11.5 billion by 2000, of which around $8.5 billion had been committed to 2,200 projects around the world.

Chief among the government's venture capital contribution is the $1 billion Technopreneurship Fund. Established in early 1999, the fund consists of three main sub-funds with the aims of supporting Singapore start-ups, developing the indigenous venture capital industry by attracting top-tier venture capital firms and establishing a worldwide network of firms investing in Singapore.

Many other options exist for funding new ventures, and there is a wealth of information for entrepreneurs available through the government's websites and offices. Government investment funds will match private investment in many cases.[18] However, only a small proportion of Singapore start-ups received traditional venture capital funding in 1999, partly because of the lack of sophistication of local venture capitalists.[19] In contrast to Silicon Valley, so-called angel investors have not played a prominent part in funding entrepreneurs in Singapore.[20]

Early adopters

Singapore's early adopters were its government-linked companies. Set up by Lee Kuan Yew's government to drive the economy forward, these have played a significant role in the development of the country since they were established in the 1960s, although their precise contribution is difficult to gauge because of the complex web of ownership and control in many cases. According to the US State Department, they contribute about 60 percent of the economy, but the Singapore government says the figure is closer to 13 percent.[21]

Lee Kuan Yew described the government-linked companies as 'new industries', providing opportunities to make entrepreneurs of some of Singapore's scholars by putting them at the helm of these behemoths. According to him, the government-linked companies spawned other companies, and the most successful were made into 'separate entities, free from ministerial control'.[22] It is worth noting, though, that the government in many cases retained ownership through a holding company.[23]

The government-linked companies provided a stable base for the growing economy, but it was the multinationals that acted as lead users and testing grounds for technology-driven products. As Hang suggests, the multinationals have the technology, expertise, global market and financial resources required to test and refine new tech products.[24]

Hard disc drive manufacturer Conner Peripherals, and later Seagate, put a different spin on the idea of a lead market. Until the early 1990s, leading hard disc drive makers would test new products in small volumes in their US markets, refine and debug the design, and then send the specifications to Singapore for mass production. The need for shortened development cycles made Conner Peripherals eliminate the home-market testing phase, shifting the process to its Singapore facility for initial testing, refinement and production, before mass production in China or Malaysia. This was an important development because it signalled that the quality of the Singapore facilities' capabilities was now comparable to that of Silicon Valley.[25]

Complementary organizations

Complementary organizations in Singapore can have as many dimensions as there are industries. In the case of the hard disc drive industry, well-documented by David McKendrick, Richard Doner and Stephan Hagard[26], manufacturers such as Seagate, Conner Peripherals, Maxtor and MiniScrib, when they first set up in Singapore, had to bring all their own equipment and train local workers up to their standards. Seagate's managers sought to lower costs by outsourcing the production of some metal parts. With the assistance of the EDB, several entrepreneurs were identified who were up to the task. Many of these had become established with the demise in 1981 of Rollei, a German firm that set up a Singapore manufacturing facility in 1970 and conducted extensive training before going into receivership. Seagate and Conner each had programmes in place to help suppliers develop.

By the 1990s, the hard disc drive industry in Singapore had evolved into a production network, with a range of specialized suppliers and expertise recognized around the world.[27]

Service infrastructure

The previous chapter described how a network of local Economy Two firms sprang up organically with the specialized knowledge to support the Economy One players. The Economy Two firms comprise the network of support services with the specialized knowledge and skills to enable the growth and development of the start-ups that form the backbone of the cluster. Although these firms almost certainly had their counterparts in Singapore to support multinationals, it can be argued that the EDB fills this role as an intermediary, ensuring that incoming and established companies in Singapore have everything they need, including a range of support services. Like law firms in Silicon Valley, the EDB also acts as a dealmaker, providing introductions and guidance, and helps with funding.

In at least one case, these elements have been provided by design.

At the Singapore Science Park, management has installed a suite of service providers including a venture capital firm, a financial services firm, a law firm, a PR agency and a management consulting firm. These services should prove welcome to local entrepreneurs since a robust professional service infrastructure for start-ups has impeded the development of Singapore's entrepreneurial ventures in recent years, according to the Global Entrepreneurship Monitor study. While this is a step in the right direction, this service infrastructure will need to expand and develop synergies with technology firms and other start-ups in order to approach the effectiveness of these businesses in Silicon Valley.

Other factors

The growth of Singapore has been achieved primarily through top-down management and direction by the government, particularly through the EDB. As a result, the path dependencies are less clear than they are in Silicon Valley. In most cases, the major initiatives were planned, executed, monitored and corrected by the state's numerous statutory boards, which seem to have been created for every conceivable purpose.

The EDB has an important role as ambassador, promoter, facilitator and supporter. Comments by company chairmen highlight its 'dedication to Singapore and its growth; optimism and self confidence; commitment to learning, adapting and innovating; strategic pragmatism and a commitment to partnering; marketing and sales philosophy built on technical competence; and a global outlook based on a sense of vulnerability as a small city state'.[28] This illustrates the success of EDB in attracting investment and cultivating growth.

Cultural considerations have also had to be taken into account. The traditional Confucian or collectivist culture is at odds with the innovative spirit that drives the entrepreneurs of Silicon Valley. Through its educational reforms and the creation of technology parks, the government is trying to encourage would-be entrepreneurs to 'think outside of the box'. But overturning deep-rooted ways of thinking may take longer than expected.

Another important element is trust, which is essential in a growth model like Singapore's that is led from the top. By following through on commitments, tackling issues fairly, demonstrating honesty and not tolerating corruption, the government gained the trust and confidence of both Singaporeans and foreign investors, who find a business-friendly and stable environment particularly attractive.

What next?

The Ministry of Trade and Industry declares:

> Our vision is for Singapore to become an advanced and globally competitive knowledge economy within the next decade, with manufacturing and services as its twin engines of growth.[29]

As with so many of its ventures, the government is putting substantial resources into achieving this objective. It is planning to encourage innovation (with the new National Innovation Council intended to 'help Singaporeans look for new ideas and new ways of doing things'); increase entrepreneurship to supplement the body of multinationals with home-grown businesses; expand the talent pool through the creation of three junior colleges, a fourth polytechnic and potentially a fifth university; continue to recruit foreign talent.

The Infocomm Development Authority is a new statutory board dedicated to providing the infrastructure needed for the transition to a knowledge-based economy. The Infocomm 21 programme includes initiatives geared towards putting everyone in Singapore online and making the country a 'premier infocomm hub' and an 'infocomm talent hub', while providing a 'conducive business and policy environment'.

Common themes, different methods

Many of the strategies and initiatives in Singapore are familiar, and it has borrowed many of them, building on and modifying them as appropriate. But it is the differences in the methods used that are more telling.

Getting noticed by the world

The driving force behind the growth of both Singapore and Dubai seems to have been gaining importance at the international level. Become indispensable and you can't be ignored. The best way to do that, as we've seen in both of these examples, is to become better than your competitors, especially your regional competitors.

Both Dubai and Singapore had to work their way out of relative obscurity, and the similarities between their starting points are striking. Both flourished as entrepôts. Lacking any substantial natural resources, each recognized the importance of developing trade and, in particular, luring foreign investment from multinational corporations with the promise of liberal trade policies and generous incentives. Foreign investors were brought into each area with careful hand-holding, and only companies that would contribute high-value-added industry were invited.

Each was made more attractive to foreign investment with the development of high-quality infrastructure. In both, companies owned wholly or partly by the government have been the stimulus for developing indigenous industries. Both have set out to become major financial centres. Singapore has succeeded; Dubai has only recently started, seemingly inspired by Singapore's example. Education has been a challenge for both, and Singapore's system is substantially more mature than that of Dubai. Both Singapore and Dubai seek to encourage entrepreneurship and knowledge-based enterprises.

Each government also seeks to lead its people and businesses by example: the development of two of the world's top e-government programmes is a good illustration of this. According to a 2001 study of 21 e-government programmes conducted by the UN, both the United Arab Emirates and Singapore rated highly, with indices of 2.17 and 2.58 respectively, compared with a global index of 1.62.[30]

Both Singapore and Dubai are strongly led. Their leaders have clear visions and ambitious plans, which the supporting government structures allow to be put into effect without delay. But it is where the two governments' methods diverge that it becomes interesting.

Top-down versus middle-out

Since his People's Action Party took power in the 1960s, Lee Kuan Yew has advocated a paternalistic, detail-oriented government, which leaves little room for ambiguity. Politically, economically and even culturally, the government of Singapore is careful to prescribe what's allowed and what isn't, down to the level of personal behaviour (no chewing gum or spitting) and restricted freedom of the press. Political dissent is carefully controlled and sometimes suppressed. Government-linked companies still make a large contribution to the country's GDP. The government has invested in large-scale public housing and has introduced a mandatory savings scheme. It's a government that likes to be in control.

Lee Kuan Yew and his successors are unapologetic about their government's no-nonsense, no-compromise policies, which, despite recent economic difficulties, have created a prosperous, well-ordered country. But the combination of father-knows-best government and traditional Asian education has created a nation of followers, not leaders, worker-bees, not innovators. Hence the Singapore government's recognition that it needs to stimulate innovation and entrepreneurship.

Whatever similarities there are between Dubai and Singapore, many in Dubai attribute much of the emirate's success to the long tradition of entrepreneurship. This is apparent at its most basic level in the Creek, where goods still flow in and out by dhow, and in the Gold Souk, with its hundreds of tiny shops. But it is also clear on a much grander scale, when the names of the prominent trading families begin appearing on all kinds of business ventures. Names like Al Futtaim, Al Ghurair, Al Rostomani, Juma Al Majid: family businesses that have built up substantial fortunes over just a few generations based on the rapid growth of trade in the area.

The government of Dubai focuses on growing the economy by creating an environment that encourages business without being too controlling. The free zones operate free from almost any type of restriction. Industries such as tourism may have been stimulated by government investment, but now market forces operate free from government intervention. Dubai lacks the 'safety net' of social services that exists in Singapore, however, and if foreign workers find themselves unemployed for any reason they seem no longer to be welcome.

In creating the stimulus for entrepreneurial growth, it can be argued that Dubai takes a 'middle-out' approach, as opposed to top-down (as in Singapore) or bottom-up (as in Silicon Valley). By undertaking projects that would be too risky for any one company in order to stimulate an industry, then stepping back as private investment begins to roll in, the government of Dubai has adopted a model that seems to be mid-way between those of our other two examples.

Notes

1 Ports of Singapore publicity (website)

2 All figures quoted in this chapter are in US dollars

3 Lee Kuan Yew. 2000. *From Third World to First*, pp. xiv–xv. New York: HarperCollins

4 Rosenberg, D. 2002. *Cloning Silicon Valley*, p. 149. London: Pearson Education

5 Wong Poh Kam *et al*. Global Entrepreneurship Monitor: Singapore Country Report 2000; available from www.gemconsortium.org

6 Lee Kuan Yew, p. 7

7 Lee Kuan Yew, p. 59

8 Schein, E. H. 1996. *Strategic Pragmatism: The Culture of Singapore's Economic Development Board*, p. 42. Cambridge, Massachusetts: MIT Press

9 Schein, p. 21

10 Lee Kuan Yew, Chapter 10

11 Schein, p. 22

12 Lee Kuan Yew, p. 68

13 Singapore Ministry of Manpower website – www.mom.gov.sg

14 McKendrick, D. G., Doner, R. F. & Haggard, S. 2000. *From Silicon Valley to Singapore*, p. 160. Stanford: Stanford University Press

15 Singapore 2002: The Remaking of Singapore – www.sg/flavour/profile_review.asp

16 Rosenberg, p. 159

17 Hang, C. C. 1999. 'What It Takes to Sustain Research and Development in a Small, Developed Nation in the 21st Century'. In *Singapore – Towards a Developed Status,* ed. L. Low, p. 35. Oxford: Oxford University Press

18 Singapore in 2001: A Review – www.sg/flavour/profile_review.asp

19 Rosenberg, p. 162

20 GEM report

21 *Business Week*, 24 June 2002, Issue 3788, p. 52

22 Lee Kuan Yew, p. 67

23 'Whither Singapore Inc.?', *The Economist*, 30 November 2002

24 Hang, p. 28

25 McKendrick *et al.*, pp. 165–6

26 McKendrick *et al.*

27 McKendrick *et al.*, pp. 165–6

28 Schein, pp. 96–7

29 www.mti.gov.sg

30 Benchmarking E-government: A Global Perspective – Assessing the UN Member States; by the United Nations Division for Public Economics and Public Administration and the American Society for Public Administration; available from http://unpan1.un.org

5 Asset creation

Companies failed to create the future not because they fail to predict it but because they fail to imagine it.

GARY HAMEL (from his book *Leading the Revolution*)

Dubai started its development with a clean slate and few resources. As such it faced immense challenges, but at least it was free to develop exactly as it chose, and in time borrowing from the experiences of others, such as Silicon Valley and Singapore. The Silicon Valley model is a bottom-up organic one. Singapore's model is led from the top. Dubai falls into a middle ground between the two, with some intervention by the leadership, as well as some organic growth.

Introduction to the models

The strategic trajectory
Dubai's experience is a lesson in how to create something where there was nothing. Dubai could still be a small, obscure emirate of no importance. Instead, it has become a vibrant, cosmopolitan powerhouse of tourism, tolerance and commerce which is rapidly becoming known all over the world. In the past three decades, the emirate has built up a range of valuable assets and it continues to do so.

This momentum driving the development of Dubai is an important underlying factor in what we call its strategic trajectory: a calculated, strategic thrust in a specific direction, with focused goals.

The Dubai model we outline borrows from systems theories that

Strategic trajectory

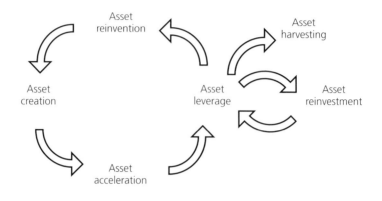

have emerged since the middle of the 20th century. Recursive and iterative, it requires multiple actors working together to create the exponential value increases that produce large-scale rapid growth. The diagram above is a graphic representation of the model.

The starting point of the model is **asset creation**, in which resources are put in place and assets – be they technology systems, intellectual property, physical infrastructure and so on – are created. In essence, something new. Of course, this kind of thing happens all the time, but on its own it doesn't explain the rapid growth of a company or economy. It's only when we place this phase into the context of the model that its strategic value begins to emerge.

Once an asset has been created, its value may go up or down depending on its output and a multitude of external factors. It's only through **asset acceleration** that we can realize greater value from its outputs than would ordinarily be dictated by market forces. The pent-up demand may be achieved by anything from infrastructural development to the accumulation of know-how or experience. These in turn will make further asset creation even easier.

Closely tied to asset acceleration is **asset leverage**, the next phase in the model. This is where pent-up demand for and the unreleased value of the asset are realized. Expertise and knowledge developed the first time round can be leveraged, and network economies begin to exhibit rapid value creation. In many cases this stage is not reached, and any pent-up value is dissipated either because of management failings or because of market conditions. This underlines the importance of astute management and reliable, real-time data gathering.

At the final stage of the model, there are three possibilities: **harvesting, reinvestment** or **reinvention**. With a mature asset that has no future value, it may be possible to redeploy some of its resources. If not, it can simply be retired. Reinvestment may be necessary if an asset is still productive but needs to be shored up, expanded or simply maintained to remain of use. Or an asset may be reinvented if alternative or additional applications for its outputs are discovered. Reinvestment or reinvention may lead to new assets being created, which brings us round to the beginning of the cycle.

The strategic vortex

Once the cycle has been completed and started again, the effect of multiple iteration and ever-increasing speed and momentum creates a **strategic vortex** (see diagram on the following page).

The combined effects of the strategic vortex result in large-scale rapid growth. As additional assets are added to the portfolio and existing assets are iterated, several things happen. Momentum increases, allowing speed to be maintained and minimizing any slowing effects from external factors. The solidity of base assets increases as they are reinvested. The scope of the portfolio of assets increases, and risk is reduced as the portfolio is expanded and diversified.

But it is a process that depends for its success on quick and effective decision-making and the ability of leaders to step back when

Strategic vortex

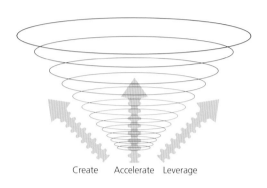

Create   Accelerate   Leverage

appropriate. Managers (or government officials, as the case may be) must choose which assets to introduce, monitor their development through the acceleration and leverage stages, and then decide whether to reinvest, reinvent or harvest. Equally important is knowing when to step back and let market forces take over; this is the only way to maximize the benefits of the leverage stage. To enable all of this to happen, two things are necessary: good, real-time data for decision-makers, and a governance structure that allows fast decisions to be made.

Going, going, gone
Many dotcoms failed because their business plans and management approach were not grounded in common sense. One dotcom that has been extraordinarily successfully is eBay. In only eight years, the company has developed an online commerce community with users around the globe, and by its own estimates it is the most popular shopping site on the internet. Since it went online as AuctionWeb in 1995 with one broken laser printer for sale, it now has websites localized for 27 countries with more than 12 million items for sale on any given day. In 2002, sales made through eBay

amounted to almost $15 billion,[1] generating a gross profit of $1 billion, two-thirds more than in the previous year.[2] Thousands of people make their living by selling goods through eBay, and bricks-and-mortar retailers also use the site to sell overstocks and factory seconds.

The company was floated on NASDAQ in 1998 at a stock price of $3 per share (split adjusted).[3] By the start of the second quarter of 2003, the stock price was approaching $90, while the NASDAQ index had fallen by over 70 percent since March 2000. eBay is successfully bucking market trends, just like Dubai, whose airline – by way of example – is growing steadily and investing billions in new aircraft despite a worldwide downturn.

The genius of eBay was that it provided a more efficient means of online auctioning than the existing methods, which were based on newsgroups and email lists that, although functional, had none of the transparency and visibility of traditional auctions.[4] This illustrates the importance of the asset creation phase. If eBay had not developed the auction software and put the technical infrastructure in place, it would not have got off the ground.

Asset acceleration followed quickly as the network of users on the growing auction site expanded by 'word of mouse': buyers would find other items of interest via searches and links from items they bought, and many were enticed to become sellers themselves. By 1997, the year that the popular *Antiques Road Show* first aired in the US, there were some 150 competing auction sites, thus demonstrating the pent-up demand for auctions.

The asset leverage phase resulted in fourth-quarter 1997 revenues of $55 million, and the company was already profitable. By that time, more than 5 million auctions had been completed on the site, and there were more than 400,000 registered users.[5] This created opportunities for learning within the company and within the extended network of traders that used the site. The synergies between buyers and sellers grew and grew.

The company's founder, Pierre Omidyar, had been involved with every detail of the company's growth and development. He was also smart enough to realize in late 1997 that he needed to bring in a more experienced management team. This kind of realization or insight often proves to make or break a growing enterprise. The business model remained solid but further investment was needed to enable further growth. Omidyar handed over to Meg Whitman, who became CEO in March 1998. This helped transform the company from a fabulously successful internet start-up led by a young techie to a fast-growing market leader run by a highly experienced management team. The company would subsequently reinvest and reinvent itself many times as the market developed, seeing off many competitors in the process. There would be asset harvesting as well, such as eBay's decision to pull out of the Japanese market in 2002.

Of course, by the time of the management change, there had already been substantial investments in new technologies, employees and other resources. This reflects the strategic vortex that began back in 1995 with the creation of the original asset, AuctionWeb. The combination of many strategic trajectory cycles has enabled eBay to become a seemingly unstoppable network of trading services, for buyers and sellers large and small.

A new way to think about strategy

Several clear points emerge from the eBay story. Management has created an environment where radical growth can take place, but the growth has occurred because of expansion within the stakeholder network. Tools and services have been developed through listening to stakeholders and watching what third parties come up with. These tools are usually much more complex ones than most individual eBay members could develop on their own. Later investments and developments have involved less risk because of the already thriving business base.

All this plays a critical part in the strategic trajectory model. What counts in the end is the ability of leadership over the long term to listen to and learn from all the stakeholders – customers, suppliers, competitors and the collective voice of the market ecosystem – and to make decisions fast.

The asset creation phase

The asset creation phase is a starting point. During a first iteration of the strategic trajectory model, it is where an idea is combined with resources to create an asset. During subsequent iterations, it may be that a new asset is created from an existing one, or something new is spun out, leaving the parent intact.

Just about any new venture or initiative could reasonably fall into this part of the model, but there are specific characteristics that you should expect to see if the assets created are to form the basis for rapid growth.

It is important to be bold, not tentative, eschewing recognized limitations to create something of real value to the growing ecosystem or strategic vortex. It is also crucial to create assets selectively and strategically, taking care to choose the ones that can grow and change over time to form a solid base for a developing portfolio of assets. To accomplish this, there must be strong leadership. Leadership underpins everything, and during the asset creation phase, vision, acceptance of risk and decisiveness are the crucial factors.

Starting with a bang

It is important to be bold, not tentative. This doesn't necessarily mean bursting out of the starting gates like horses at the Kentucky Derby; it may mean taking risks or being an industrial heretic, or just setting off with a new idea like eBay did in 1995. This marks a distinct difference between this model and the organic model that emerged in Silicon Valley over decades. If you want rapid growth it is crucial to start with a bang, because there isn't time to wait and see what develops. This is particularly true when coming from behind, when there are established competitors to contend with. In these cases, there is the potential to leapfrog the incumbents, so it's even more important to make a strong start.

It's equally important not to be deterred by potential constraints but to acknowledge and overcome them. For example, Dubai Internet City was conceived, planned, built and launched in a year, a fraction of the time it would have taken in many parts of the world. It is now a key component in Dubai's portfolio of assets, attracting foreign investment and workers, facilitating knowledge transfer and contributing to Dubai's international standing as an emerging technology hub. The Palm Islands were born from the need to overcome a limitation: a shortage of coastline. Even though they are years from completion, the Palms are already contributing to the world's perception of Dubai as an innovator and an attractive tourism destination. Although the vast amount of planning and study that went into each of these examples shouldn't be minimized, they are typical of the bold strokes being made on the canvas of Dubai by its leaders.

In the words of Anis Al Jallaf of the Dubai International Financial Centre:

> When you believe in something, go for it. Don't hesitate. When you're flying a plane, put the full thrust into take-off. Burn half the fuel tank. Once you're airborne, then you're fine.

Choosing key assets

The initial assets created underpin everything else that comes after; so, just as it's crucial for skyscrapers to be built on solid foundations, the initial assets must be the right ones. They must be able to develop and they must contribute to the vision behind the drive for growth. The choice of new assets to be developed must not be whimsical or random or merely to take advantage of a short-term opportunity. Decisions motivated by such forces simply divert resources and management attention from where they are most usefully employed.

Timing is also crucial. In Dubai, for example, there is a long history of creating assets as part of the process of anticipating or even creating demand. Most of the large investments made by the government since the 1960s were attacked by critics who said there was no demand for them. But they have since proved successful: the demand emerged or was stimulated. Recent examples of good timing include the Dubai International Financial Centre. There now appears to be a demand for a robust, well-regulated financial market, and as a late addition to Dubai's portfolio, it should complement other thriving industries and flows of capital. This will be an interesting project to juxtapose the financial market's need for control and regulation against the free-market, anti-bureaucracy approach of Dubai.

Sheikh Ahmed, Emirates Group chairman, makes the following point about the combination of vision and timing:

> We believe that you have to put supply before demand. If you wait until demand exists, you may be too late. Go wherever your vision leads you, and the business will come through good business practices.

By remaining focused and developing the right assets at the right time, the business ecosystem can sustain itself through periods of rapid growth and it can remain intact in times of difficulty. Raja Easa Al Gurg, managing director of the Easa Saleh Al Gurg Group, a prominent, diversified family-owned business in the emirate says:

> Dubai is like the water of a river. Sometimes, a big stone will fall into the river, but the water will go around the stone. Dubai is like that. Even with all the regional problems in the 1990s, Dubai was at its peak. Dubai is well-established, with good foundations, and the government knows exactly where it's going.

Communicating a vision

Unlike many so-called corporate visions that amount to little more than a motto or slogan, the vision of the leadership in Dubai seems to be widely understood. Generally, it is about transforming the emirate into a magnet for tourists, workers and corporations from around the world based on high-quality facilities, infrastructure and way of life. There have been various explicit vision statements, including those expressed in Dubai 2010,[6] which sets out the following targets for 2010:

☐ Dubai will have become the symbol of what a knowledge economy can achieve.
☐ Dubai will have become emblematic of a mindset of innovation, dynamism and entrepreneurship. It will be synonymous with high added-value creation, high-tech and a spirit of excellence and integrity.
☐ Dubai will be the benchmark showing how a well-implemented strategy focused on the optimum use of existing and new assets, on well-defined positioning and on the impact of 'networking power' can create successful new businesses both large and small.

Anwar Gargash, executive director of Gargash Enterprises, an old and established family business, says:

> You can see the vision of Dubai going back many years. You see it reinforced by Sheikh Mohammed, but the rulers have always been visionary and very focused. Sheikh Rashid was very focused on trade and re-export. His sons have focused on different areas as times have changed.

Talking about Sheikh Mohammed, Abdulhamid Juma, chief executive of Dubai Media City, says:

A lot of people cannot understand the relationship we have with His Highness. Knowing him or not knowing him is not the point. He gives you a lot of energy just by being around.

As he articulates them, Sheikh Mohammed's goals for Dubai are humble, but they provide an indication of his leadership style. When asked how he would like to see Dubai perceived around the world, he replied that he would like people to have heard of it. He then added that he would like Dubai to be a place where people are happy, where they enjoy their work, their lives and their families. And as simple as it seems, it is clear that the emirate is being managed with precisely these goals in mind. For this reason, it is little wonder that this vision is so widely known.

Accepting risk

Another important part of effective asset creation is accepting the risk that goes with it. Seeming to fly in the face of a level of risk that would deter others has been inspirational in Dubai; and every time the risk has paid off, there has been a strengthening of confidence in the leadership and its vision. As mentioned above, the high-risk projects undertaken in Dubai before an obvious business case may have existed have helped to solidify both the Dubai vision and confidence in its leadership.

Indeed, risk-taking appears to be a crucial part of the government's role, as family-owned businesses in Dubai are famously risk-averse. Sultan Bin Sulayem of the Dubai Ports, Customs and Free Zone Corporation related one example. Sheikh Mohammed approached a group of ten family-owned businesses, offering them the opportunity to develop a large swathe of land between the Creek and the airport into a theme park. After protracted discussions among themselves, the families were sceptical about the potential of the investment. So they returned to Sheikh Mohammed and asked if they could develop the area with 75 percent in property and the remaining 25 percent as a theme park.

They were given the go-ahead but failed to agree on how to proceed. The area is now being developed by Emaar Properties as a massive mixed-use development known as Dubai Marina, which is about one-third government-owned.

Sultan Bin Sulayem is circumspect about the government's role as a risk-taker in Dubai:

> If the government waits for someone to build the Dubai Marina, it will never happen. If Sheikh Mohammed waits for someone to build the Palm, they will look at it and keep thinking: 'Should I do it? Is this a good investment?' But now that the government has taken the risk, all the traders are investing because it is already becoming successful.

Raja Easa Al Gurg echoes this point from the merchant's perspective, saying that they 'can't stay in a tent and watch the tall skyscrapers being built all around'. The results show that the government's strategy is working. By investing first it reduces the risk for others, who then invest when they find conditions sufficiently attractive. Despite the risks taken by the government and a long history of entrepreneurship in many forms, Dubai may find its growth hampered if some of the stigma associated with failure is not alleviated. As in Singapore, but markedly different from Silicon Valley and much of the West, failure in business inevitably entails a 'loss of face', the prospect of which may prevent some from starting new ventures. As new sources of capital emerge, this reluctance to fail may begin to wane as entrepreneurs become less reliant on funds from their families and friends, and failure leads to less personal consequences.

But rapid growth need not always involve living on the edge. As a portfolio of assets grows, the risk profile of the portfolio stabilizes, and new assets can be created with substantially reduced risk. An example is the second Palm Island, where all the feasibility had already been completed and demand was proven. Of course, it still involved risk, but it was much less than for the first Palm Island. Moving a step further, this also means that new assets can be introduced with a much higher degree of risk because their failure would not be catastrophic to the business ecosystem.

The Earl of Home has been involved with Dubai since the 1960s while at merchant bank Morgan Grenfell, when he helped engineer the financing for building Port Rashid, the first hospital and many other projects. According to The Earl of Home, early projects were so large, relative to the resources available to the government at that time, that the failure of any one of them might have bankrupted the country. But he also stresses that even a project like the Dubai International Financial Centre, although large and important, presents less risk to the emirate than early major projects.

This has less to do with the importance of the financial centre than with the solidity and diversification of the asset base that has been developed in Dubai, which is such that the failure of one project, even of this magnitude, could be easily absorbed by the ecosystem. Of course, such risk can never be completely eliminated, particularly in the context of very large projects like this or, say, the Burj Dubai, announced in May 2003 and planned to be the world's tallest building. The Burj Dubai will take its place on Sheikh Zayed Road among newly constructed parkland and open spaces, incorporating a hotel, residential apartments, office space, leisure facilities and one of the world's largest shopping malls. When completed, the building will be taller than Malaysia's Petronas Towers (452 metres) and the yet-unfinished Shanghai World Financial Centre (expected to stand 492 metres).[7] In another bold move, the world's largest shopping centre is being planned for a site adjacent to the Burj Dubai.

As Dubai extends into the ocean (with the Palm Island developments) and into the sky, it seems to be embracing risks that would prove unacceptable to many, fully expecting that these projects will ultimately prove technically feasible and commercially viable. Mohammed Ali Alabbar explains the reasons behind the tower:

Dubai is keen on being on the world map. There's a lot of competition around creating the tallest buildings, so that is another opportunity for Dubai. At first, Dubai was competing regionally, now we compete globally.

Which, of course, means that the risks increase, but Dubai appears eager to meet these risks head-on.

Being decisive

Vision and being unafraid of risk are of little use if the decision-making process is cumbersome and slow. You must be able to identify and implement new projects and roll them out quickly, because if you wait too long you may be too late to benefit from the opportunity. In Dubai, Sheikh Rashid's government went ahead with large infrastructure projects despite scepticism. His son, Sheikh Mohammed, has done the same.

Managers involved in these projects recall what happened when Sheikh Mohammed gave them the go-ahead. A solid business case was presented, after which he simply told them to begin. In the case of Palm Island, Sultan Bin Sulayem was given the green light while driving one evening with Sheikh Mohammed. He could scarcely believe it and asked for clarification. The reply came: 'I told you to go ahead with Palm Island. Let's start.' The project team has remained as lean as it was at the start, with just Sheikh Mohammed, Sultan Bin Sulayem and a couple of finance people and engineers as the only decision-makers.

A hotel-group senior officer reinforces how important this straightforward approach is:

It's the leadership that makes things work here, and it's simplicity. The simplicity of the connection from somebody saying 'do it' to somebody who will start and get the job done. Dubai has the ability to get things done very quickly because the lines of command are very clear and straightforward.

Asset creation in Dubai

There are many examples of strategic asset creation in Dubai (see below). In most cases, they differ from similar projects elsewhere in the region in that they are indeed strategic, each taking its place in the formation of Dubai's strategic vortex and helping to strengthen the asset base. Neighbouring countries have begun staging conferences, developing property and organizing sporting and other events, and these are frequently very successful on their own. But they invariably appear to be one-offs that neither work towards a cohesive vision nor consistently strengthen the country's brand name internationally. By contrast, Dubai's strategic management of its assets and their cohesive marketing domestically and internationally make each initiative appear to be part of the emirate's grand plan.

Port Rashid

Dubai's origins as a port and trading centre are the cornerstone of its success. After the modernization of the Creek showed the potential for Dubai as a shipping hub, Sheikh Rashid began planning for a new man-made port near the centre of Dubai. Following a series of studies between 1965 and 1967, plans went ahead to build a deepwater free port with four berths near the mouth of the Creek. Many of the design features of the proposed port, including the free port model, were based on benchmarks, notably the highly successful free ports in Singapore and the Netherlands. When the project was well under way, Sheikh Rashid and his advisers became anxious. They wanted more berths because the booming trade in the area indicated that four berths might not have been enough. So Sheikh Rashid told the engineers to increase the capacity of the new port to 16 berths. This is a good illustration of the decisiveness that is so important in the asset acceleration phase.

However, the change in plans came at a price; the cost of the 16-berth port was estimated at about $32 million (equivalent to about $142 million today). Despite the recent discovery of oil, Sheikh Rashid sought to cut costs wherever possible. The engineers had planned to construct the two large breakwaters from imported stone, but Sheikh Rashid suspected that there was a local source. He had heard that nomadic people had experienced difficulty in digging wells in remote areas of Dubai, so he commissioned a study to determine whether any potentially useful material existed there. Sure enough, a deposit of limestone was found that would provide enough material for the breakwaters and several other future projects as well. Using local stone shaved almost one-third off the original cost estimate. When the project began to fall behind schedule because of delays in trucking the limestone to the site, the ruler is said to have demanded 24-hour deliveries, routing the clamorous trucks past his palace to save time.

The port was officially opened in 1971, and its 16 berths were immediately put to use. Sea trade in the area had grown massively since the project began, so Dubai's new port was a welcome and valued addition. Of course, this was not the end of the story. Further indications of growth led to expansion of the port to its current capacity of 35 berths and the creation of the much larger Jebel Ali port.[8]

Port Rashid was the first of several large projects to be put in place by Sheikh Rashid and his successors. As such, it is a good example of asset creation for the strategic trajectory model. It built on an existing competency in the region and involved committing huge resources in anticipation of future demand. The strategic value of the port was substantial. It opened just as demand in the region was at an all-time high and neighbouring ports were oversubscribed. This not only brought a lot of business to Dubai, it also helped to raise Dubai's profile and reputation among shippers, traders and other countries in the region.

It was the largest project ever undertaken in Dubai. If the initial design had seemed risky based on two years' worth of studies, the revised plan with four times the capacity must have seemed like madness to some.

Despite the unprecedented size of the project, it was completed quickly. This was made possible by the ruler's decisiveness and facilitated by a system that allowed decisions to be implemented immediately. All this was helped by the ruler's frequent presence on the site, enabling him to keep in touch with progress and deal with any problems that arose.

Sultan Bin Sulayem describes Dubai's philosophy toward development and the role of the ports within it:

> The philosophy the government has for Dubai is to provide facilities before the business opportunity comes. It is very critical to Dubai's expansion. We are pioneers. And if we target our business, we don't say 'I'm going to provide these facilities but you have to sign this document that you are going to use it'. This is what would happen in many countries. Not in Dubai – we take a chance. We say, if we provide facilities, opportunities will come.

Jebel Ali Free Zone

Sheikh Rashid is regarded with reverence and admiration throughout Dubai, and his leadership set the stage for the emirate's development. An indication of the fondness Dubaians still have for Sheikh Rashid is the proliferation of anecdotes about him that are heard almost anywhere. One concerns how he identified the site where Jebel Ali Port and Jebel Ali Free Zone would be built. Apparently, he was walking on the beach and stuck his staff into the sand, declaring that spot the ideal site for the huge development. When surveyors and engineers turned up later to complete the feasibility studies they confirmed his view, and that is where the port and free zone were built. The accuracy of this story is less significant than its popularity, reinforcing the commonly held affection for him and placing the development of the Jebel Ali area in the context of Sheikh Rashid's vision for Dubai.

Jebel Ali Free Zone was established in 1985 on a site adjacent to the Jebel Ali Port. The object was to attract international investment by companies that would benefit from proximity to the port and the ability to operate independently of the UAE's employment and company ownership regulations. Freedom and ease of doing business formed the basis of the value proposition at Jebel Ali Free Zone from its earliest days. Freedom to hire whoever you like, to manage your finances and assets as you like and to set up almost any sort of enterprise you like.

Establishing a business in the zone is eased considerably by a kind of corporate concierge service, which helps investors with all aspects of setting up and operations, including obtaining permits and licences and even building premises.

The project got off to a shaky start with only 35 companies investing over the first couple of years, but the zone is now home to around 2,300 companies. According to one senior manager involved from the start, 'we evolved an industry by building an infrastructure for industry'. This infrastructure has been a big selling point for many of the investors in Jebel Ali and other free zones.

Because of UAE regulations, though, companies cannot set up shop inside the free zone to sell directly to the domestic market. A partnership with an exclusive local 'agency' is still required for that. So, for example, although Sony has a large warehouse in the free zone, it supplies a company in Dubai that has the exclusive local distributorship.

The import and re-export business has been a mainstay for the free zone, but the infrastructure has allowed manufacturing, services and other industries to prosper since the zone was established. Furthermore, the thousands of workers (over 90 percent foreign, by one estimate) employed there contribute to the local economy by renting housing, using services, consuming utilities and buying from local businesses.

The free zone is another important strategic asset. It fits with the vision of transforming Dubai into a world-class commerce hub. The goods were flowing in and out of the port, and it was a natural next step to allow companies to operate freely in the same area.

Since the free zone was created only after Jebel Ali port was thriving, risk was lessened, as would be expected as further assets are created over time within the scope of the expanding strategic vortex.

The free zone concept has since been used in a variety of contexts in different industry concentrations in Dubai. Some examples of this are examined later.

The Jebel Ali Free Zone is a good example of how Dubai creates assets despite apparent constraints. It also helped communicate and reinforce Sheikh Rashid's vision, focusing on making it easier for foreign companies to invest and do business in Dubai.

Emirates

Emirates is a young airline, established in 1985. Again, it is a strategic addition to Dubai's portfolio of assets, making a similar contribution as Singapore Airlines has made to its home country. By the mid-1980s, the ports were booming, international companies were setting up in the free zone and the economy was in good shape. The airport had been operational for a quarter of a century and was used by the regions' then-dominant airline, Gulf Air, and other international carriers.

But even though the UAE had no national airline until then, there was already airline experience in Dubai thanks to Dnata, a travel services company originally established in 1959 to provide ground handling and ticketing services. With a virtual monopoly on cargo management and ticketing, Dnata was known as an airline without any planes. Today, it is part of the government-owned Emirates Group along with the airline. Employing over 4,500 people, Dnata still manages many of the operations at Dubai International Airport and has a successful IT spin-off, Mercator.

When the government resolved to start its own airline, the management team at Dnata already had the skills to do the job. Dnata's head, Maurice Flanagan, who was on secondment from British Airways, was approached by Sheikh Mohammed and asked to start a new airline with an initial investment from the government of

$10 million. It was not a lot of money with which to start an airline, particularly one which was meant to be self-sufficient and not to come back for more handouts, and which would have to compete under the airport's open-skies policy, which exposed Emirates to competition from much bigger established airlines.

In addition to the experienced management team from Dnata, Sheikh Rashid's young half-brother, Sheikh Ahmed, was appointed chairman at the age of 25. He took up the role with enthusiasm after completing his education in the West. Maurice Flanagan recalls giving him a series of tutorials on the airline industry:

> And increasingly those tutorials turned into an equal dialogue … several times a week; the sort of dialogue you would expect between a very switched on, active, involved chairman and his chief executive.

Emirates started with a small fleet of leased planes, and its first routes connected Dubai, Mumbai, Karachi and Delhi. Now Emirates is the world's fourth most profitable non-US airline and the 21st largest in the world. Maurice Flanagan attributes much of this success to the necessity of surviving without subsidy. At the start of 2003, Emirates flew to 64 destinations. It had 44 wide-body planes and another 70 on order.

The airline's growth plans are co-ordinated with the government's plans to increase visitor traffic to Dubai, ensuring that as visitors numbers grow, there will be sufficient hotel rooms, seats on Emirates' planes and capacity at the airport.

When it was hatched in the mid-1980s, Emirates was a necessary piece of the puzzle that would help underpin Dubai's growing importance as a business centre. Over time, it has become a key component in providing access to the city as part of the larger strategy that includes the development of the tourism industry. Additional economic benefits are the jobs it provides and the contribution it makes to the local economy.

1960s – Dubai and the Creek

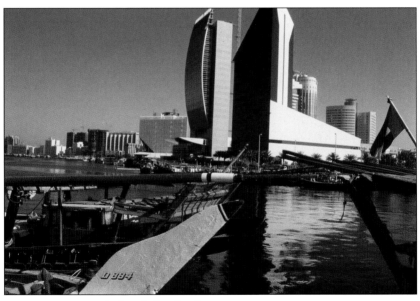

21st century – Dubai and the Creek

1960s – The site of the existing Jumeirah Beach Hotel (an oil storage construction facility at the time)

21st century – Jumeirah International's hotels: the Jumeirah Beach Hotel and the taller Burj Al Arab, the world's only seven-star hotel

1950s – Dubai immigration

2003 – Dubai International Airport's duty free section

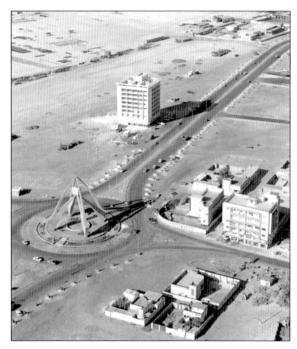

1970s – Dubai landmark, Clocktower Roundabout

21st century – Dubai landmark, the Palm Island

The airline also serves an important function as an ambassador for Dubai. Its levels of service are among the best in the world, and its approach reflects a high degree of professionalism. Emirates is a strategic asset that has been developed as an increasingly important component of Dubai's portfolio of assets. The ability of its managers to work together and make decisions fast has been crucial, but a large part of its success is due to the fact that it has to be profitable and competitive and does not have the umbrella of subsidy and protection that some national airlines enjoy.

Emirates had the advantage of starting with a blank slate. Mike Simon, director of communications, reckons that this was a major reason for the airline's success. In building the airline from scratch, those in the initial management team (most of whom are still with Emirates) were able to draw on their experience and avoid mistakes they'd seen in the past.

The experience available to Emirates was not limited to its management expertise. The history of immigration and trade with the Indian subcontinent made routes connecting with Pakistan and India obvious early choices for Emirates, with every chance of the airline being able to run those services at close to full capacity. So the risk involved in creating the airline was reduced by building on the existing platform of collective industry experience and a strong knowledge of the initial markets.

The Palm Islands

There is no better illustration of asset creation today than the Palms: two identical palm-tree-shaped islands being built up from the sea bed off the coast of Dubai. The project reflects all the hallmarks of strategic asset creation: thorough planning, rapid execution, groundbreaking scope, flexible parameters and hands-on leadership. It's part of the government's plan to lure 15 million tourists per year to Dubai by 2010.

Already visible from space, the two landmasses and the crescent-shaped breakwaters that protect them are taking shape in the Gulf as the world's largest dredgers help construct the islands from rock and sand. When completed in late 2005 and 2006, the Palm Jebel Ali and Palm Jumeirah will have more than 5,000 residents (not including visitors), around 80 hotels, sports, leisure and shopping areas, and over 12,000 palm trees. The cost of land reclamation, infrastructure and landscaping is estimated to be around $3 billion for both islands (not including private or commercial building development).

The project grew out of a need for more beaches for the increasing numbers of sun-seeking tourists. Among the ideas for adding to the coastline was extending the landmass into a series of islands. As this concept evolved, it began to take on the shape of a palm tree. Eventually, the Palms will lengthen the coastline from 72 kilometres to 192 kilometres, an increase of 166 percent. The Jumeirah Palm will measure about 5 kilometres in length and width, and the Jebel Ali Palm will extend about 2 kilometres further along each dimension. Each will also have a crescent breakwater providing shelter from the open sea and more space for development. The Jumeirah Palm's breakwater will measure about 11 kilometres in length and Jebel Ali Palm's will measure about 15 kilometres.

A land reclamation project of this magnitude had never been attempted before, and the government of Dubai wasn't about to take any chances. So 50 separate studies were completed by 42 different consulting firms to investigate the feasibility of the project and the implications for the environment and economy of the region. Once the results were in after four years of planning and study, Sheikh Mohammed announced the project in May 2001. Construction of Palm Jumeirah began the following month.

Sultan Bin Sulayem is head of the Palm Islands project. He explains how they approached the inherent risk in a project of this magnitude:

> We prepared all the ingredients for success before we started. But speed is very important. Because opportunities are true only if you

catch them at the right time. Otherwise, you might be ready, but people will not be interested. So we took risks. But we believe there are always bigger opportunities when you take risks. And if there's no risk at all, everybody is doing it.

Sultan Bin Sulayem is talking about the Palms, but also, more generally, about Dubai's approach to risk. With his responsibilities extending across all of Dubai's ports, free zones and customs operations as well as the development of the Palms, he might be expected to sit behind a desk and rarely make an appearance in the field. But this couldn't be further from the truth. He is a frequent visitor to the Palm sites to check progress, and he even learned to scuba dive in order to be able to inspect the progress of the geotextiles that make up the new landmasses. On a late-night excursion to one of the sites, on his own in a small boat, he found that the landfill had progressed further than he'd expected. The boat became stuck and he only narrowly escaped being blasted by one of the computer-controlled nozzles that shoot sand into place using satellite guidance.

Sultan Bin Sulayem's close involvement with the project has allowed it to evolve and change as it goes along. The first release of 2,000 residences on Palm Jumeirah sold out within three weeks while the designs were still on the drawing board. When the initial designs were completed they were criticized, so, despite the engineers' protests, he had them changed.

The initial plans did not include building all the residences; plots were to be sold and buyers would be responsible for building their own homes. Sultan Bin Sulayem began to have second thoughts about this while staying in a development in California. The undeveloped plots were unsightly, and the noise of one-off building projects here and there was a nuisance. Based on this experience, he recommended to Sheikh Mohammed that an additional phase be put in place in which all the residences would be built.

The ability to be connected to the day-to-day progress of the project and make decisions fast is a crucial element of success for Sultan Bin Sulayem, and one reason the time required to execute large projects like this can be compressed:

> When you collect all the information on a project, then you have some control on your destiny. You have some control on timing. You have some control on success. And that is what we do on every project.

And how are the decisions made? Easily, according to Sultan Bin Sulayem:

> We are not bureaucratic on the Palm Island project. We only need a few people to make any decision. With any tender, I do the analysis with a finance person and my engineers, then we take the recommendation to Sheikh Mohammed. It takes me ten minutes. I tell him, 'This is the project, these are the costs, this is the timing and this is our recommendation.' And he says, 'Go ahead.' His go-ahead is verbal. Then we do it, and we do it fast. If we have to make a change, we do it. I have total authority – if everything has to come to somebody, we'll never finish.

This method seems to be effective. As of the start of 2003, the project was running on time and to budget.

The creation of the Palms has strategic value for Dubai as a tourist attraction in itself, in addition to the individual hotels, restaurants, shops and leisure facilities that will be built on the islands. It will also provide thousands of beach-front residences for the growing population of Dubai residents, now including expatriates, who until recently were not allowed to own property.

The government is funding the project, along with the UAE and international banks, assuming substantial risk, not only financial, to develop an asset from which many sectors of the economy will benefit. In one go, the project more than doubles Dubai's beach area, adds housing, entertainment, leisure, sports and retail facilities, and, most importantly, adds another superlative asset to Dubai's existing portfolio.

The project management and decision-making processes are similar to those that have been used in other large-scale projects. Management is involved at all levels and is able to make decisions immediately, thus avoiding the chance of any problems that arise getting out of control or delaying progress.

In the context of other developments in Dubai over recent years, the Palms seem to fit in naturally. But imagine if those running your organization were able to cast aside any perceived limitations (like a limited coastline, or the daunting prospect of manufacturing a small city on mounds of sand in the ocean). What breakthroughs might result?

Creating the key ingredients

A number of elements emerged in Silicon Valley that many believe were essential to its growth. They were introduced in Chapter 3 and revisited in the context of Singapore in Chapter 4.

A supply of workers

As in Singapore, Dubai had little to work with at the start, apart from a trading culture, a willing population and strong leadership. These three components remain important. One of the principal selling points of Dubai's free zones has been the freedom to bring in workers without complex immigration regulations. But although the free zones offer benefits, such as 100 percent ownership for foreign firms, which are not allowed outside the zones, it appears to be reasonably easy to get a work visa with the promise of employment for most foreigners. The difference inside the free zone is that the 'concierge' service helps with and fast-tracks this process. Inside the zone or outside, foreigners are not welcome in Dubai if they are not working or making a positive contribution to Dubai's economy.

Nevertheless, most companies setting up in Dubai must bring in skilled workers from abroad, simply because the indigenous pool of talent is too limited. One of the value-added services provided by Dubai Internet City is assistance in recruiting. Recognizing the importance of bringing in outsiders to fill posts, the government of Dubai actively promotes the cosmopolitan, liveable qualities of the area – as well as the tax benefits – to entice skilled workers to move there.

Dubai has also been able draw on a pool of labour that many neighbouring areas cannot, will not, or have been slow to use: women. Female UAE nationals and foreigners alike are welcomed into the workforce with a degree of freedom virtually unheard of elsewhere in the region. Apart from the cultural and historical reasons that were discussed earlier, the government actively encourages women to take part in the economy. Indeed, women are assuming increasingly important roles in the public and private sectors, in ever greater numbers. In addition to proactive government initiatives geared towards creating opportunities for women, prominent businesswomen such as Anita Mehra Homayoun, Raja Easa Al Gurg and Sheikha Lubna Al Qasimi make a point of acting as role models.

Early adopters and lead users

Another essential ingredient is the presence of early adopters and lead users in the economic ecosystem. The US military filled this role in Silicon Valley, and large government-linked companies in Singapore did so in that country. This is not dissimilar from the approach in Dubai, with the large projects undertaken by the government. The big difference is that the government of Dubai sets out to break records and explore uncharted territory. Then it invites competitors from around the world to get on with the work.

By setting high standards and assuming risk too great for any private enterprise, the government drives innovation and attracts the best of the best to figure out how to meet its ambitious goals.

The Palms development is an obvious example. The scale and time-frame of the project are unprecedented, so the engineers and designers have had to stretch their capabilities and develop new ones to get the job done. These new capabilities will remain in Dubai after the project is completed, augmenting the experience of local contractors who work with the foreign firms enlisted to do the work.

Service infrastructure and complementary organizations
These elements lead naturally to the creation of two more key ingredients: a service infrastructure and a network of complementary organizations. A business network has been in place and growing for over half a century in Dubai because of its strength as a natural port and its pro-trade policies. The stimulus the government has provided for the creation of new industries has also resulted in entirely new networks.

In the construction industry, architectural and engineering firms are often brought in from abroad to design and manage large projects, but the rest of the capabilities required seem to come from a growing pool of local providers.[9] The equestrian industry also shows how a sophisticated web of supporting and complementary providers can emerge in response to a developing market.

Within the free zones, a network of businesses has formed to support the variety of industries within them. In the Jebel Ali Free Zone, for example, there are all manner of logistics and shipping equipment supplies and services, providing businesses with a wide choice of suppliers for virtually anything they require. Services inside the zone include a chamber of commerce, international banks, insurance companies, consultancies and real estate firms. Essentially, everything an investor might need lies within the gates of the free zone. The ease of setting up business in the free zone and market requirements have clearly contributed to the creation of this robust business ecosystem, but the Jebel Ali Free Zone Authority also makes a point of helping its investors, satisfying any need that might arise. In many ways its role within the free zone is similar to that of Singapore's Economic Development Board.

Networks like these are also developing rapidly within the newer free zones. In Dubai Internet City, for example, more business seems to be conducted among the companies inside the zone than with outside customers and suppliers. Companies such as Microsoft and IBM, in particular, work hard to develop suppliers and partners inside Dubai Internet City.[10] Tejari.com, a home-grown business-to-business exchange kicked off by a government initiative, is based in Dubai Media City. The company works with many suppliers inside Dubai Media City and Dubai Internet City (both part of the same free zone area). Sheikha Lubna, the company's CEO, attributes much of the success of the business network to the free zone's management, which actively tries to get companies together to develop business.

Venture capital, local universities and R&D

The remaining two ingredients, a dynamic venture capital environment and world class local universities and R&D, have been slower to emerge in Dubai. But recent government initiatives are under way to overcome these shortcomings.

The relatively unsophisticated financial markets in the UAE have produced little venture capital to fuel entrepreneurial growth. Although the entrepreneurial tradition in the region dates back to the earliest days of traders along the Creek, ventures have been financed by organic growth and the reinvestment of profits. Thus trading families that became wealthy during the middle of the 20th century have become involved in new industries. Nevertheless, trade remains a mainstay for many of them. There has also been little incentive to enter the venture capital market because of the absence of the straightforward exit route, something that most venture capitalists would expect.

Recognizing these difficulties, the government has established a $190 million fund as part of the Mohammed Bin Rashid Establishment for Young Business Leaders to help young entrepreneurs get businesses off the ground. The programme also offers incubator-like services, including advice, connectivity, premises, training and a network of recommended suppliers. This is only a drop in the ocean, of course. Although the Dubai International Financial Centre will focus on attracting institutional investors, the resulting emergence of Dubai as an international financial centre can also be expected to pave the way for the growth of a native dynamic venture capital industry, as awareness, sophistication and comfort levels grow.

Lastly, the government of Dubai has recognized the importance of creating local top-class universities and centres for research and development. Initiatives taken to address current concerns include the Knowledge Village and Dubai Silicon Oasis, which are part of a plan to create a knowledge-based economy. By mid-2003, plans to develop a business school in partnership with a top-tier, internationally recognized business school were under way. Several foreign universities have already set up campuses or programmes in the emirate, and plans for several graduate and postgraduate level programmes are in the pipeline. Developing high-quality, internationally recognized educational institutions will take time, of course; in the meantime, students continue to go abroad for university and postgraduate study.

The most significant transfer of knowledge to the local population takes place in the workplace. Attracting the world's most innovative companies to Dubai allows UAE nationals to work alongside and learn from skilled workers from abroad. The Knowledge Village development adjacent to Dubai Internet City has already attracted the interest of many international training and e-learning providers, who are eager to serve the growing community of knowledge-hungry workers in Dubai.

In all these cases, the government has developed the principal components for growth and then allowed them to develop naturally. When more capital is made available for entrepreneurs and appropriate facilities for higher education and research and development are created in Dubai, the emirate's portfolio of assets will be complete and will be able to fuel further the momentum of the strategic vortex.

Notes

1 Ebay company information – http://pages.ebay.com

2 Ebay year-end results for 2002, from press release, 16 January 2003

3 www.shareholder.com

4 Hapgood, F., 'Bidder Harvest,' *Inc.*, *1997 Inc. Technology*, Vol. 19, Issue 13, p. 58

5 'Auctioneers ready for prime time?', *Inter@ctive Week*, 9 February 1998, Vol. 5, Issue 5, p. 53

6 Presented by Sheikh Mohammed at the Dubai Strategy Forum 2001, taken from abstracted presentation provided by The Executive Office

7 Emaar Properties press release 21 May 2003

8 Description of the creation of Port Rashid summarized from Wilson, *Father of Dubai*

9 From an interview with Charles Neil, Dubai International Financial Centre

10 From an interview with Ahmad Bin Byat, director general, Dubai Technology, Electronic Commerce and Media Free Zone

6 Asset acceleration

We must use time as a tool, not as a couch.

JOHN F. KENNEDY

The next phase in the strategic trajectory model is asset acceleration. Less tangible and less obvious perhaps than the other components of the model, this phase might be compared to elastic potential energy in the study of physics. It can be described as the coiling of a spring, which creates increasing amounts of potential energy as it is compressed. The energy is realized when the spring is released.

Assets can create the potential for a huge burst of commercial activity when conditions reach the right point. This acceleration can happen in many ways and at many levels. The announcement of a new product can create demand that results in the product selling out on its launch. On a larger scale, tourism in Dubai has grown hugely over the past decade through a combination of many assets: hotels, attractions, Emirates and Dubai International Airport, as well as clever marketing and great service. In either example, it is important to recognize the management role. The product might have sold out without the pre-launch marketing, and Dubai's tourism industry might have grown on its own, without careful co-ordination and marketing. But to achieve dramatic asset acceleration, a catalyst must be introduced and managed.

In the context of the strategic vortex, it is important to remember that the acceleration of one asset will depend on the state of the business ecosystem at the time it is introduced, so a new asset will benefit from the base assets and the synergies that already exist. The greater the size of the assets in play, the greater is the risk; but risk can be mitigated as the strategic vortex develops. Some risk might also be avoided by relying instead on a slower and less predictable organic route to growth.

This concept becomes clearer when regarded as a precursor to the next phase – asset leverage – where explosive growth is realized. In Dubai, there has been one prominent factor and three aspects of strong leadership that have enabled such explosive growth. Persuading people and companies from all over the world to come to Dubai has had a natural acceleration effect on its own, stimulating competition, learning and collaboration. The leadership has created an environment that allows acceleration to happen by instilling confidence at every level, replacing regulation wherever possible with mutual trust and balancing control with freedom of action.

Aspects of asset acceleration

Welcoming the world

Inviting outsiders into Dubai, which has few natural resources, makes sense. In a region where many view foreigners with a degree of suspicion, Dubai has long taken a contrary view, believing the presence of outsiders helps trade thrive. This is reflected in the population of the emirate, where fewer than one in five are UAE citizens.

By welcoming the involvement of foreigners, Dubai's economy has benefited in many ways. High-profile projects have attracted a wide range of skills to the area, and Dubai is now a recognized source for highly skilled workers and managers. Their skills may have been developed abroad, but they have been honed on cutting-edge, fast-track commercial and residential building projects. These projects involved top-class companies from around the world, which competed keenly for the chance to participate. An example is the Palm Islands development, as Sultan Bin Sulayem explains: 'It's unique. Everybody wants to be involved in something historic.' The dredgers needed for the massive earth works, for example, were brought from the Netherlands.

Historic or not, the accumulation of skills combines with best practices from around the world to benefit further development. UP Tower, a 54-storey residential building on Sheikh Zayed Road, was completed in less than 18 months despite numerous technical challenges and is fully occupied. A fast-track process was used for construction, allowing a floor to be completed every three days during the most productive periods. As well as the extremely tight completion deadline, further difficulties were introduced by the small 30 × 30 metre footprint allowed for the structure, making it one of the slimmest skyscrapers in the UAE. To overcome these constraints, contractors used fast-track building techniques that were introduced to Dubai during the building of the neighbouring Emirates Towers complex. Elements of the structure were redesigned and many were pre-made offsite. The importance of co-operation and co-ordination among the multitude of contractors on a project of this size meant that hundreds of skilled engineers, construction workers and other specialists were able to learn new techniques, which they could then use on future projects.[1]

The high proportion of expatriates helps create and reinforce high standards, as Ahmad Bin Byat, director general of Dubai Technology, Electronic Commerce and Media Free Zone, explains:

You come here for access to talent. This is one of our key successes. It's a melting pot of good and very skilled people. Even if he's a cleaner, he's going to be the very best because he wouldn't be here otherwise.

Because of the high mobility of the immigrant workforce it's very competitive, and unemployed people cannot remain in Dubai unless they are contributing to the economy in other recognized ways. This may seem harsh, but it acts as another force in raising and maintaining standards. Dubai's agency laws were designed to help bring outside expertise and investment to the emirate. By requiring foreign investors to take on a local partner owning at least 51 percent of the business, the regulations appear to have accomplished their initial goals. Local traders have learned a lot from their partners, and many have grown wealthy in the process. Raja Easa Al Gurg's family business based its early success on working with foreign investors in this way, but now she finds opportunities elsewhere, particularly in the free zones, which are attracting a new breed of wholly owned multinational competitors:

> We are learning from the free zone enterprises because they're new, and whenever anything new comes, you have to consider what the impact on your business will be. We can't just depend on the companies for whom we are agents.

The accelerating effects of opening Dubai to the world are readily apparent in the free zones. In Dubai Internet City and Dubai Media City, over 1,000 companies have been licensed in only two years. At the airport, the open-skies policy has helped to attract airlines from all over the world. In the hotel industry, the growing trade in tourism and conferences has attracted investment from the world's leading chains.

Instilling confidence at every level

Throughout the strategic trajectory model, leadership plays an important part. For asset acceleration, one component of leadership is instilling confidence. This works on several levels: the individual, the organization and the business ecosystem.

Seemingly impossible deadlines are invariably met because the ruler gives those in charge of projects the confidence to do it. Sheikha Lubna describes her experience of the e-government project and the Tejari.com exchange:

When Sheikh Mohammed gave us 18 months to launch the e-government portal and two months to launch the exchange, I was so scared I couldn't tell him. It was a public announcement. But I had a great confidence boost because of him. He developed that in me. He pushed me beyond my boundaries.

Sheikh Mohammed confirms his strategy, stressing the importance of remaining at arm's length:

I give people the confidence to complete a project, but they can't succeed if I'm standing right on top of them. Leadership is giving people the courage to succeed themselves.

How can Dubai's leadership instil this confidence? The key seems to be that people must have genuine confidence in the leaders. When Emirates Group's Maurice Flanagan explained the fast growth of the airline and airport, he reinforces this point:

Because of Sheikh Mohammed and Sheikh Ahmed, it all happens at a pace you would not find anywhere else in the world. It needs that push, and probably more than anything else, absolute confidence in the authorities behind it to make it work. This is exceptional, and I don't think you'll find it anywhere else in the world.

Confidence is also important in a much broader sense. Tourists must be confident that Dubai will be a good, fun, safe holiday spot that offers value for money. Investors need confidence that the government and the economy are stable. This has never been more important than with the advent of the Dubai International Financial Centre, where success will hinge on the world's confidence in its new regulatory framework and the quality of its executive management. The government's record of investment in Dubai, it seems, has gone a long way towards creating much of the confidence that investors want to have.

Confidence in itself can create potential value. When people believe that they can make breakthroughs, they are more likely to do so. And when customers or investors become confident in an opportunity, their money will soon begin to flow.

Replacing regulation with trust

The need for regulation in the Dubai International Financial Centre to gain the confidence of the international financial community is at odds with the apparent lack of regulation that has brought so many investors to Dubai. The trading community has thrived on trust. But what has been good enough for traders has not been enough to encourage growth in the region's capital markets, so regulation in the financial centre will be needed to help create the same level of trust and confidence in the system. Creating this sense of trust, using regulation where appropriate, is another important aspect of leadership for the asset acceleration phase of the model.

Keeping regulations, restrictions and red tape to a minimum helps maximize opportunities for interaction among the players in the system to create value. (Think of the restrictions imposed by the agency laws to see the opposite effect.) It also allows things to happen more freely and quickly, since there are fewer impediments to change or growth.

As with so much of the ingrained culture in Dubai, this comes back to the generations-old traditional trading culture. With little enforceable regulation, early traders were only as good as their word and their last transaction. Any swindlers would be shunned and unable to trade in the Creek. 'Trick me once, shame on you; trick me twice, shame on me', says an old Arab proverb. Unscrupulous traders generally never got the chance to trick twice.

Things are not so different today, as Shehab Gargash, director of Daman Securities, explains:

When you have a trading port, you have a trading code. It's

probably unwritten. When you have a trading code, everyone knows his rights and obligations. You've got your honesty; you've got your commitment to deals and your word. Today, that's supported by documentation and letters.

Anis Al Jallaf, chairman of the Dubai International Financial Centre, learned this as a teenager, watching how business was done in his brother's shop in the 1970s.

My brother used to import silverware. I used to tell him how funny some of it looked to me, but he would tell me that it was made for a specific area in Iran. So one day, an Iranian man came in and liked the silverware so much, he asked to buy every piece my brother had. That was two containers. But the man didn't have money with him. He asked if he could take the two containers, then bring back the cash when they were sold. My brother said, 'no problem'.

'No problem?' I asked. I couldn't believe it. My brother told me that he knew the man's father, and he was honest, so his son should be honest. My brother believed he would come back, maybe in two months, maybe in four months, maximum six months. It had a lot to do with simplicity. My brother said, 'I look at his eyes, and I read him, and he doesn't look funny.' A lot of business happened that way.

If letters of credit and official documentation had been required to do this deal, it would have never been completed. This example shows the continuing importance of trust and reputation in the trading community. Anis Al Jallaf also passionately argues against letting the dishonest few dictate regulations for everyone:

We cannot have a law that cripples the honest 99 percent just because one percent have done wrong. We have to work on how to detect that one percent and punish them.

Dubai Media City's Abdulhamid Juma believes that this system works:

> I don't have to wonder if companies here are cheating me.
> Everybody is okay until proven otherwise.

Trust between the rulers and their lieutenants is clearly important. It's no coincidence that the same names appear repeatedly at the heads of high-profile projects. The rulers trust certain people to get the job done, and then they're rewarded with more responsibility. It's also clear that the business community trusts the government. Of course, this is closely tied to the sense of confidence that the government creates. It also creates trust through its fair treatment and follow-through on commitments. Khalid Bin Sulayem, director general of the Department of Tourism and Commerce Marketing, points out:

> Even in the worst of times, Dubai has done well. That's why people have full trust in Dubai: because of the history.

As Dubai grows, civil servants advocate more regulation, which the merchant community argues against. There have even been incidents in which new regulations have been put in place then retracted by the government after an outcry from the business community. But high-profile examples, such as the loss of over $200 million by Dubai Islamic Bank in 1998 resulting from the actions of dishonest employees, make it clear that there are always some people prepared to take advantage of the trust which underpins the business environment.[2]

So the challenge is to create an environment where inherent trust exists but is buttressed by sufficient regulation to keep the business and financial sectors upright. Charles Neil, secretary to the board of the Dubai International Financial Centre, talks of the objective to create 'a 21st century economy, with little but good regulation, minimal bureaucracy, visionary leadership and a drive in people to succeed'. This is consistent with Sheikh Mohammed's often-articulated desire to prevent over-regulation from stifling Dubai's growth and development.

Maintaining control
In the asset acceleration phase, leaders must set the right balance between control and freedom of action. In many societies, controls and regulations have increased, sometimes stifling business growth or individual creativity. Even Singapore has accepted that it needs its people to be more creative, and the challenge will be achieving this in the shadow of long-established customs and government policies.

Dubai's method of control is through informal networks, based on trust and ethical norms; it is not regulation-based, as in most developed countries. It works in Dubai because companies are closely held and the network of leadership is extremely tight; those who stray from accepted practices soon find they have no future in the emirate. This ad hoc method of control has proved flexible and able to cope with the rapid change Dubai has experienced. Creation of the free zones shows how an intelligently controlled operation can increase available freedoms instead of restricting them. Within the free zones, the management issues trading licences, provides services and acts as a one-stop local government for the companies within them. In the highly specific legal structure of investors' tenancy agreements and the infrastructural and managerial powers retained by each zone's management, a substantial amount of control exists. But the companies inside the zones actually benefit from much greater freedom than they would elsewhere in the UAE.

An intelligent management approach that exercises control while allowing considerable freedom of action will increase the rate of asset acceleration by providing the ability to tweak and adjust as necessary without stifling growth. In sailing terms, which seem appropriate for a country that owes a lot to the skills of its dhow traders, it is the equivalent to a light but firm hand on the tiller to ensure that everyone moves in the right direction as quickly as possible.

Asset acceleration in Dubai

In each of the examples examined below, an existing asset has been accelerated through intervention of some sort, and then grown through asset leverage. It is important to remember that acceleration occurs on many levels. Even without 'catalysts', a degree of pent-up value would almost certainly be created, through either organic growth or the influence of other assets in the system.

Open skies and the airport

Only a few decades ago, Dubai's airport was not much more than a local airfield, virtually indistinguishable from other regional airports. In 1969, nine airlines served 20 destinations from Dubai. The airport has since been transformed. In 2002 it handled 16 million passengers, 18 percent more than in the previous year. Over 100 airlines operate out of Dubai, serving 250 destinations. The airport is now the main hub for air travel in the Middle East and a major stopover point for passengers continuing from Europe to the South Pacific and other long haul destinations.

The open-skies policy, originally put into place by Sheikh Rashid when the airport was first opened in 1960, has been a major driver in attracting so many airlines from around the world. Even in the 1950s, when air travel was only for the privileged few, Sheikh Rashid had ambitions to make Dubai a major air hub. To kick-start this plan, the open-skies policy ensured that any airline could begin flying to Dubai without the need for international treaties or bilateral agreements.[3] At the airport's inception, Sheikh Rashid was so confident about its prospects that he had a 500-space car park built next to the single air strip and small terminal, telling Dubai and those willing to listen that great things lay ahead.

By eschewing the protectionism that has held back air travel in many parts of the world, Dubai has seen its passenger traffic grow over fourfold and its cargo traffic twelvefold since 1980. This growth has occurred hand in hand with increasing the capacity of the airport itself. With passenger numbers expected to reach 30 million by 2010 and 45 million by 2030, expansion and improvement are continuous. In 2000 a new terminal was opened, and a $2.5 billion expansion project will ultimately increase capacity to 60 million passengers per year, compared with 22 million in early 2003.

The open-skies policy created massive asset acceleration for the airport. The more airlines allowed in, the more planes will come; and the more planes there are, the more cargo and passengers there will be. It's as simple as that. While the open-skies policy on its own has no direct economic effect, it serves as an accelerator for increasing imports by air, business travel, stopover traffic and tourism. The policy is analogous to Dubai's free trade and relaxed immigration policies. It all comes back to the ruling family's oft-expressed credo: 'What's good for business is good for Dubai.'

Anita Mehra Homayoun, director of marketing and corporate communications at the Department of Civil Aviation, calls the airport the 'window to Dubai'. She goes on to describe how passenger traffic fuelled further growth:

> Most of our passengers in the 1980s were transit passengers, and they began to notice the great duty-free facilities in the airport. Our intention during that time has been to 'wow' people with the quality of the shops compared with the ones at other airports in the region.

This demonstrates how, over time, increased demand has been created through word of mouth and return visitors, building a competitive advantage for Dubai.

The open-skies policy also stimulated innovation and competitiveness, as is often the case in the asset acceleration phase of the model. Emirates might have been the first one to cry 'unfair' when it was established in 1985 and was expected to compete with much bigger established airlines already flying out of Dubai. In fact, it was the requirement to compete and be self-sufficient, the need to learn and improve, that made Emirates succeed; and it has been profitable in nearly every year of its existence.

When Dubai began to be used by long-range aircraft, a new emphasis was put on the range and quality of its services, facilities and duty-free shopping. The Dubai Airport Cares programme was put in place to co-ordinate the way the airport authority, airlines, customs, security, duty-free concessions, shops and other organizations and their employees dealt with customers. According to Sheikh Ahmed, the message is:

> You may belong to someone else's department or have a different boss, but you must believe that this is your airport, and forget about who your boss is. Ignore all of that, and remember that we are as one.

The education programme designed around this initiative is meant to instil a confidence and professionalism in all airport workers that passengers will notice.

The airport and its duty-free facilities have received several government service awards, which Khalid Al Kassim, assistant director general of planning and development at the Department of Economic Development, believes help create confidence among shoppers:

> You see government awards in the airport for excellent service, and you will trust them and you will trust that you are buying good products and that you'll get good after-sales service.

In maintaining the open-skies policy at Dubai International Airport, the government preferred to rely on trust rather than regulation in turning the airport into a dynamic transport hub. Sheikh Ahmed explains:

> We found that the more you are flexible with the airlines, the more likely they are to want to come here and fly to other points. And as they become a user of the airport and the traffic goes up, others will also try to connect because you are creating that competition. Then airlines will feel more confident going to a busy airport than to an empty one.

The confidence that continues to attract air traffic to Dubai is the essence of asset acceleration.

Tourism and hotels

Tourism has acted as a major accelerator for the hotel industry in Dubai since the early 1990s. Growth in tourist numbers is related to the growth of Emirates and the increasing capacity of the airport. Each of these assets develops within its own strategic trajectory while gathering momentum and feeding off the growth of the others.

The number of hotels increased from 70 in 1990 to 272 in 2002, and dozens more are being planned or being built. Between 1990 and 2001, the number of visitors to Dubai for business or pleasure increased from 1.7 million to 3 million, and occupancy rates averaged 57.2 percent (with lows in the early 1990s because of the Gulf War).[4]

One prominent hotelier describes the implicit agreement between entrepreneurs and the government. The government encourages investors to build new hotels, even when hotels seem to be springing up everywhere, with a promise that tourists will arrive to occupy them. To keep its promise, the government ensures that Dubai tourism is adequately marketed and that the airline and the airport are equipped to handle the traffic. Then, as more visitors arrive, they spread the word about Dubai, leading to further increases in visitor numbers. Raja Easa Al Gurg describes how the government invests to raise the profile of Dubai:

> They don't think just one or two years ahead. When they built the Burj Al Arab hotel, they didn't think they'd get their money back in two years. They thought of how many times the Burj Al Arab would be seen around the world, and how many people would come to Dubai to see it.

Indeed, Jumeirah International's properties often appear to be much more than hotels. The Burj Al Arab, the Emirates Towers and the Jumeirah Beach resort are all landmarks that present formidable challenges to incoming competitors.

The hotelier mentioned earlier described his experience of opening a 600-room luxury hotel in early December 1997 and his surprise at seeing it become fully booked that Christmas. It was an indication of the pent-up demand being created. He recalled going to Europe and finding that almost no one knew much about Dubai; he realized what potential for tourism there could be if the travel logistics, infrastructure and accommodation were first class.

Some of the high-profile hotels have been built by the government rather than by private investors. Their success has encouraged other hotel chains to enter the market. The resulting competition and the innovation spurred by the need for the new assets to stand out from the crowd are typical of the effects of the asset acceleration phase of the model. Such government investments help make new investors sufficiently confident to enter the market, and Dubai now has one of the fastest-growing portfolios of luxury hotels in the world. Virtually every major chain is represented, with each new entrant striving to outdo the last.

Events and conferences are also important in creating the asset acceleration effect. The Dubai Air Show and other major events, as well as international conferences, help fill the hotels and make other contributions to the local economy. Trade shows have accelerated development of corporate apartments, hotels and the new Dubai International Convention Centre.

The acceleration effect extends beyond Dubai's borders. Sharjah, a neighbouring emirate, has become more conservative over the past decade, arguably as a response to the influx of Western tourists to Dubai. In Sharjah, women must dress traditionally and alcohol is no longer served. Oil-rich Abu Dhabi, the capital of the UAE, remains conservative but does not object to bikini-clad women sunning themselves on Dubai's beaches. Qatar, however, appears to be seeking to emulate Dubai's successes by developing shopping centres, hotels and an airline, creating festivals and events to lure tourists, and promoting sporting events.

Dubai Internet City and Dubai Media City

Dubai Internet City and Dubai Media City are two free zone developments within the Technology, Electronic Commerce and Media Free Zone. They are highly valuable assets developed in line with the government's strategy to diversify its portfolio and become a knowledge-based economy. They are also good examples of how asset acceleration has taken place as a result of the synergies between the companies within the zones. In this case, the 'corporate concierge' services provided by the management of the zones have been a strong catalyst in creating this acceleration.

The origins of the two developments are typical of large-scale projects in Dubai. The idea started with Sheikh Mohammed, who became interested in immersing Dubai in the so-called new economy in the late 1990s, when the dotcom boom was roaring ahead. Studies commissioned by his office revealed that the two most attractive industry clusters to promote were information technology and media. At that time (and, indeed, today), the Middle East represented one of the fastest-growing markets for IT, so that was an obvious choice. Media's appeal owes a lot to the freedom of expression enjoyed in Dubai relative to some other states in the region.

The Jebel Ali Free Zone had shown that Dubai was an attractive location for multinationals. To determine exactly what would lure technology and media companies to the area, government representatives surveyed a number of large companies. The results were not surprising: the top priorities included freedom of ownership and financial management, no restrictions on hiring from abroad, and a solid technical and communications infrastructure.

Once the studies had been completed, Sheikh Mohammed set aside an area 35 kilometres from the city and imposed a one-year deadline for completing the first phase of Dubai Internet City, including finding tenants to occupy it. To the amazement of many, Dubai Internet City was opened on schedule in October 2000 – one day early, in fact – with 85 companies in residence and a long waiting list. Dubai Media City was launched three months later.

By early 2003, after only about two years, the Technology, Electronic Commerce and Media Free Zone had licensed almost 1,100 companies (621 in Dubai Media City and 470 in Dubai Internet City) on a site covering 1.5 million square feet. In late 2003, it was announced that the total area of the zone would be expanded to 5 million square feet[5] and would include retail, leisure and residential properties as well as offices.

Within the zone where the two cities are located, firms can enjoy full foreign ownership, no restrictions on repatriation of capital, no currency restrictions, tax-free status for 50 years and freedom to hire who they like. There are also stringent intellectual property and so-called cyber regulations in force. In short, as with the Dubai International Financial Centre, there is regulation where it is needed – in this case to protect intellectual assets – but otherwise firms are given a pretty free hand. This is why so many companies have set up in the free zone. Outside it they would be subject to UAE agency laws, requiring any foreign company to take on a local partner with a controlling interest in the business of at least 51 percent, which is not an attractive proposition in comparison. From the perspective of visitors, the distinction between Dubai

Internet City and Dubai Media City isn't readily apparent. The most obvious clue that you're in Dubai Internet City is the giant @ signs on every building and much of the signage. Many buildings also bear the names of large companies such as IBM, Cisco, Reuters and CNN; which camps these fall into is clear. But there are other examples that are not so easy to place, such as Mastercard and other financial services companies. There are also dotcoms such as Tejari.com, a business-to-business exchange, in Dubai Media City. Because it's all part of the same free zone, the same regulations and benefits govern companies in both areas.

The stated mission for Dubai Internet City is:

> To create an infrastructure, environment and attitude that will enable Information and Communications Technology (ICT) enterprises to operate locally, regionally and globally from Dubai, with significant competitive advantage.

Providing the infrastructure is the easy part. Creating a business-friendly environment is more difficult, and it's where many would-be Silicon Valleys around the world have fallen short, often ending up as little more than office parks. This is where asset acceleration comes in, enabled in large part by the 'corporate concierge' service provided by the management of both Dubai Internet City and Dubai Media City.

Part of this service focuses on relieving companies of administrative tasks such as incorporation, real estate management, visas and licences, and voice, data and satellite communications. The management of both cities will do whatever it takes to allow their partners (as they call their tenant companies) to concentrate on doing business. Other services provided by the management are geared towards enabling partners to work with one another and helping them get new business, which helps to generate the asset acceleration effect.

To create synergies inside and get business from outside, Dubai

Internet City groups companies by industry focus and then invites major buyers from those sectors to workshops, where contacts can be made and potential opportunities explored. It also arranges for company representatives to attend relevant trade shows in promising locations.

The services provided for these companies bolster their confidence through association with, and the support of, the management of the two cities. The support encourages firms to make marketing efforts, such as visiting a trade show, that they might not otherwise have contemplated. As part of the Dubai Internet City community, they have more visibility and legitimacy. And not just in terms of outward appearance or marketing spin: the network effect enhances what the companies in the community have to offer.

Tejari.com's Sheikha Lubna is enthusiastic about many aspects of her company's position in Dubai Media City. Her employees enjoy working in a safe, well-maintained, attractively landscaped office park among technology and media people. But she is also quick to put the role of technology in its place when she says that Dubai Internet City exists

to drive transition and transformation for people … in business. It's not the techies who are important here. It's what these techies are going to do for the rest of the community.

This idea is reinforced by Abdullatif Al Mulla, general manager of Microsoft's regional office in Dubai Internet City:

The whole concept of Internet City is when you need something, you know where to go. Internet City is a hub, where anybody looking for something to do with IT knows where to head … If I'm looking for partners, I don't have to email anyone or look for negotiators. I just meet, and we finish on the spot. So the proximity helps us a lot, and increases the flow of communication.

As one of the first companies to sign up to Dubai Internet City and a relatively large operation, Microsoft works actively to cultivate suppliers and partners. Abdullatif Al Mulla describes the benefits for companies large and small within the city as completely reciprocal, with large companies needing the smaller ones as much as the small ones need big ones like Microsoft. He also describes the difficulty in finding good people to work at Microsoft, but this isn't a problem unique to his regional office, it's one experienced throughout the company. Like most companies in Dubai Internet City and Dubai Media City, Microsoft recruits from around the world through agencies and websites, thus adding to the extremely diverse population of the free zone. Since the majority of companies and their employees are foreign, the diversity of the group creates its own synergies as people from vastly different backgrounds come together to compete and collaborate with one another. They are open to the world's companies and its workers.

In the common areas of the two cities it is clear that the developments are much more than an office park. Like the lobby of the Emirates Towers Hotel, they are constantly buzzing and crowded with business people having meetings or waiting for appointments. The main area of Dubai Internet City is alive with visitors chatting while sitting in comfy armchairs or at the espresso bar with a view of the man-made lake, with the management's busy staff of around 500 visible through a glass wall in their open plan office. The asset acceleration inside the zone is evident in several ways: the fast take-up of office space and the waiting list for it, the demand for housing, leisure, and retail facilities within the site, and the amount of business done among partners within the zone. This effect has also brought Dubai closer to the larger value proposition of becoming a knowledge economy.

When the idea for Dubai Internet City was first conceived, Sheikh Mohammed compared it with the business environment of the Creek,[6] but it's already become much more than that. Through the initiative of the management of the two cities, companies of all sizes have become part of a thriving network of businesses and extended their marketing reach far beyond the borders of the UAE. Abdulhamid Juma sums up the accelerating effect of Dubai Internet City and Dubai Media City and their management services:

> To be very honest, we did not expect such demand. Maybe it's because we have talked to the companies. We did not know what to offer, so we ran workshops to find out what the companies want. They wanted infrastructure as number one. They wanted Starbucks as number two, for some reason. Then breaking down red tape and making things work. The one stop shop: I do everything for you here. I call it the package.

Conclusion

There are many different facets to the asset acceleration phase, but they all contribute to the creation of greater value that can be released later on. The open-skies policy at Dubai International Airport allowed airlines from all over the world to come to Dubai which created the foundation for the airport's growth. The building of massive numbers of hotels has been fuelled by an acceleration effect from the growth in visitor arrivals. And the bundle of services provided by the Technology, Electronic Commerce and Media Free Zones has caused demand for real estate in Dubai Internet City and Dubai Media City to grow beyond all expectations.

In each of these cases, innovation and competition were spurred by the interactions between companies and individuals from all over the world. The speed of both change and growth has been fostered by an underpinning of confidence and trust between customers and suppliers. Controls and regulations have been put in place to enable further value creation rather than stunting it.

The acceleration effects of these and other players in Dubai's strategic vortex over time are described by Anwar Gargash:

You can't go into fourth gear unless you've already shifted through first, second and third. This is how Dubai constantly raises the threshold. Other regions that try to compete with Dubai have to build up infrastructure and quality of life. A cumulative process is essential to accomplish this; it's taken many years for Dubai.

Next, we'll see how the value generated in the asset acceleration phase is released, often with dramatic effect, in the asset leverage stage.

Notes

1 Gulf Construction Online, April 2002, Vol. XXIII, No. 4
www.gulfconstructionworldwide.com

2 Economist Intelligence Unit, Country Profile 2002, *United Arab Emirates*

3 Wilson, *Father of Dubai*

4 Department of Economic Development, *Development Statistics of Dubai 2002*

5 www.blonnet.com

6 From an interview with Abdulla Majed Al Ghurair and Avi Bhojani

7 Asset leverage

Just as there can be but one Singapore; Dubai must be distinctive in what it wants to be, and there will be but one Dubai.

JOHN QUELCH in discussion with SHEIKH MOHAMMED

Asset leverage picks up where asset acceleration leaves off. In this stage, radical growth results from the acceleration effects of the previous stage. To return to the analogy from physics, it is when potential energy becomes kinetic or actual energy. Knowledge is used to create something fantastic, synergies become productive, competition creates innovation. This is where the real growth happens in an asset which, when combined with the growth of other assets within the strategic vortex, leads to the kind of results achieved in Dubai.

Asset leverage is about using the interactions among an existing portfolio of assets to create – through innovation, competition and collaboration – radical growth and development.

Compared with the top-down growth model in Singapore, where the government keeps a tight rein on many aspects of life and work, and the bottom-up organic growth model of Silicon Valley, the Dubai model is middle-out. The leadership guides the business ecosystem, intervening and stimulating here and there, then steps back and lets things happen. When things do happen, first comes asset acceleration followed by asset leverage. As most parents are aware, knowing when to let go can be difficult. Most parents like to keep a close eye on their children's progress and to offer guidance and help when it is needed.

Asset leverage occurs at multiple levels. Similar assets can leverage one another within an industry cluster. Groups of assets can work together on a large scale. As leverage begins, the interactions in different parts and different levels of the ecosystem spill over into other parts and levels. Since the Dubai Shopping Festival was conceived in 1996, it has grown by leaps and bounds. The asset acceleration has been created by good marketing: first within the region, then internationally and all the time within Dubai. Because the festival lasts only a month, there are another 11 months each year during which acceleration can build, to be leveraged when the festival begins. Apart from the retail boom, the spillover effects of the festival are clear: hotels are full almost to capacity, and restaurants, tourist attractions and related services all benefit from the people who come to Dubai for the festival. This success of the festival has also helped launch a range of sporting events during the same period and has spawned the Dubai Summer Surprise, focusing again on the regional Middle Eastern market.

This spillover effect is illustrated by an example Sheikh Rashid used many years ago to explain why the airport was important to Dubai. A man arrives at Dubai airport on his way to a meeting in the city. He buys a pack of gum and gets into a taxi for a ride into town. He pays the taxi driver, who uses the money to buy fuel. When the traveller arrives at his hotel, he orders a cup of coffee. Later, he goes out and finds a present for his wife, and so on.[1] This is basic economics at work, but it goes to the heart of asset leverage. One additional visitor to a country like Dubai will benefit the local economy in a variety of ways. Multiply this effect by the number of additional visitors who are continually attracted to Dubai by the growing asset base and the power of asset leverage becomes increasingly clear.

Mike Simon of the Emirates Group gives another illustration of the spillover effect of asset leverage:

Three or four months after we started to fly to South Africa, I was walking round the centre of Dubai and there was a Woolworths. It had just opened. The Woolworths was not Woolworths UK, it was Woolworths South Africa and I thought, this is so interesting because it reflects what we always say in that we bring commercial ties between two countries when we start to fly there.

Sultan Bin Sulayem provides another good example of two sorts of assets leveraging one another.

If you look at the port and free zone, the port definitely makes more money because the free zone is limited as to how much it can make. But the port isn't. But also, the free zone generates business for the port. When you have a port and a free zone, you maximize profit. Because the free zone generates the business, the port handles the business, and you make money.

This example shows how collaboration between two assets can create disproportionate benefits.

Key components of asset leverage

The key components of asset leverage are:

☐ the ability to take advantage of asset acceleration, the natural precedent to leverage;
☐ timing;
☐ understanding how to combine assets for maximum effect;
☐ the ability of leadership to empower workers;
☐ the ability of leadership to step back and give market forces a free rein.

Using asset acceleration

As noted in the previous chapter, the value generated by asset acceleration can happen on its own through natural market factors, but the most dramatic effects are seen through the application of a catalyst. Asset leverage can also happen organically, not following on from asset acceleration. In either of these cases, growth will depend on the behaviour of the market and reactions of the assets in question.

Removing barriers to and encouraging trade are big spurs to asset acceleration, which in turn will increase growth, particularly spillover growth, achieved through asset leverage. When a country is open to the world, word of mouth travels faster, the mix in business ecosystem becomes richer and networks expand exponentially. Dubai Ports Authority's expansion into the management of foreign ports and free zones is a good example of this. The authority could only have become known around the world as a result of shipping lines spreading the word. The more new firms that come to do business in Dubai, the more innovation among companies there is.

The leadership attributes that are important in the asset acceleration stage continue to be important in asset leverage. Trust and confidence in the business ecosystem and those who inhabit it are crucial as growth continues, and as different types of assets leverage one another. Although freedom of action will also undoubtedly contribute to faster growth, it needs to exist within a stable, controlled environment and be supported by regulations that prove necessary for reasons of business confidence and trust.

Indeed, the ability to intervene when necessary will become increasingly important as growth slows, opportunities for spin-offs present themselves, or other reasons for intervention emerge.

Timing

Judging when to introduce a new asset into the system, or when to shift from acceleration to leverage, is crucial. Even Dubai seems to get it wrong sometimes, as in the decision to set up the Dubai Ideas Oasis dotcom incubator in Dubai Internet City.

Other decisions have been much better. Mike Simon explains:

1985 was a good time to start an airline. I don't think you could have created an airline that's become as successful as Emirates at another time.

The emergence of Dubai on the international business scene in the 1980s was one positive indication of the timeliness of this decision. Asset acceleration of the airline began almost immediately, allowing a quick transition into the leverage phase as the airline began acquiring its own aircraft and expanding its routes.

Dubai's rulers are well known for their desire to shave time off development and building processes, but the people around them seem to have developed a knack for living up to these expectations. Examples are Sheikha Lubna's fast work on Tejari.com and the e-government portal launch, the one-year development of Dubai Internet City and the fast development of the Palms project. The rulers seem to have developed a knack for identifying opportunities that need only to be announced in order to generate massive amounts of accelerated value. The first Palm Island attracted a great deal of interest from the earliest planning stages, then sold out in days. Dubai Internet City, too, gained buy-in almost immediately from the likes of IBM, Microsoft, Oracle and others. By making the time these projects take to complete as short as possible, asset leverage can begin while the excitement is still fresh and has not been dulled by a long development stage.

Stepping back

The leaders' role is to set the stage, make sure an asset is in place and functioning well, and show that demand for it exists. Then they should step back and let others take advantage of the acceleration that has built up behind it.

In Dubai the rulers provide a lot of support for new industries, but on a strict 'sink or swim' basis. Mike Simon of the Emirates Group explains:

We're given a free hand and we're run just as an ordinary commercial concern. We're not protected, and we're not given any subsidies. I think that's how Sheikh Mohammed likes all businesses to go, even those in which the government has a big investment. He believes in open skies … a good example of where the government is hands-off and it's sink or swim – if it works, good; if it doesn't, close it down.

As the original owners of all the land in the emirate, the rulers often kick off a major project by handing over some real estate, as in the case of the Dubai International Financial Centre and similar developments. Although the ruling family often invests its own money in projects, developers usually have to fund their projects through local and international banks, as would be expected in most parts of the world.

Ahmad Bin Byat of the Dubai Technology, Electronic Commerce and Media Free Zone describes the brief negotiations with Sheikh Mohammed in planning Dubai Internet City:

We got the land from the government and we came back with our wish list, which really had a lot of things to do with freedoms to do things the way we wanted to do them. His Highness was very keen on giving us this, but also he gave us a bigger challenge. 'Fine,' he said, 'you can have these freedoms, but I'm not giving you any money to do it. And let's see if we could make this work as a commercial project that could stand on its own.' That was really a challenge.

Because of the success of the project, it has remained free of any government subsidy or support. The entire Technology, Electronic Commerce and Media Free Zone development doesn't cost the government a penny; it has its own police, infrastructure, planning and road construction crews. As Ahmad Bin Byat puts it, 'It's like running a whole country – a tiny little country.'

The government's laissez-faire policies aren't always appreciated, however. Property owners complained when new property development led to rents going down, but the government left the rates to market forces.

Empowerment

Giving individuals the skills, confidence and resources to work independently is important in asset leverage. Sheikh Ahmed describes Sheikh Mohammed's tendency to do this:

> He is the main driver behind pushing everybody. He is pushy, he is aggressive, he wants things to happen yesterday if you decide today, but also at the same time, he gives you all the support you need. Not like somebody who asks you for something and does not give you the support – financial, moral, or whatever – you need to make it happen. He will push you to do things, but he will always be there to support you.

Microsoft's Abdullatif Al Mulla draws parallels between the empowerment culture in Dubai and his company's hiring practices:

> The key to good management is having people you can trust. You empower them because you believe in their capabilities. I'm not going to hire anybody that might hurt my company. I'm going to hire a person to help me, to collaborate with me, to co-ordinate things with me. So what we do is hire people that we can rely on and people that we trust, that we know will treat the company as their own. The same thing happens in Dubai. They hire people, and the more they trust them the more jobs they give them, the more projects they can handle.

Asset leverage in Dubai

The previous chapter looked at a number of examples of asset acceleration in Dubai. Below we examine the asset leverage phase and how it has created growth, competition and innovation.

Hotel innovation and growth

The effects of the asset acceleration of the hotel industry in Dubai can be seen in the growing numbers of tourists and convention visitors coming to the city, and the influx of leading hotel chains. Mike Simon describes how the government stimulated the industry, then stepped back:

> The government gives a lot of support in the comfort zone area. They always encourage people. When they wanted hotels to be built here they came in first and built some. Then local businessmen were encouraged and believed they could afford to invest and make some money.

Dubai has one of the highest concentrations of luxury hotels in the world. By the end of 2002 it was home to 272 hotels with over 23,100 rooms, and more than 20 new hotels with at least another 5,000 rooms are scheduled to open between 2003 and 2005.[2] This does not include the 80 hotels with 8,000 rooms planned for the two Palm Islands. But it's not just a numbers game. The government invests in hotels that give Dubai international prominence, and private investors have to compete with those hotels. The Burj Al Arab was intended to set a standard that's nearly impossible to match. The world's only seven-star hotel, as some describe it, was designed to resemble the full sail of a ship, and at 321 metres, it is the world's tallest hotel.[3] It is composed of luxury suites, and each floor has its own reception and a staff of butlers. So spectacular is the atrium (also the world's tallest) that many tourists are happy to pay the admission charge just to be able to look at it. The hotel even has an underwater restaurant that's only a short internal submarine ride away.

The Burj Al Arab is one of the government-owned Jumeirah International's properties. Others include the Emirates Towers (the third tallest hotel in the world, with the world's largest floor mosaic in one restaurant), the Jumeirah Beach Hotel, with its own man-made coral reef, and the Jumeirah Beach Club complex.

The Royal Mirage, operated and 50 percent owned by Kirzner International (previously known as Sun International Hotels), a leading developer of resorts, hotels and casinos, was extended in 2002 after opening only three years earlier, more than doubling the size of its beachfront grounds. The new buildings at the resort, designed to look old and traditional, were constructed using largely local materials. The resort also has the largest swimming pool in the Gulf region.

The superlatives are not limited to Dubai's top hotels. The otherwise unremarkable 20-storey towers of Marriott Executive Apartments are linked by the world's longest footbridge. The 73-metre bridge connects the 19th floors of the two matching towers. The buildings were opened in January 2001, and the bridge was completed two years later, turning an ordinary pair of apartment buildings into a world-record holder.[4]

Jumeirah International has also founded the Emirates Academy of Hospitality Management in association with the Ecole Hôtelière de Lausanne, a leading Swiss school of hotel management. The academy offers a four-year BSc in International Hospitality Management, which includes study abroad and work experience at Jumeirah International's properties.

The development of the hospitality industry in Dubai has been the result in large part of government initiatives in promoting Dubai and upgrading facilities. These helped to create asset acceleration, which, in turn, resulted in asset leverage: more hotels and more innovation.

This shows how the strategic vortex works at several levels. Dubai's portfolio of hotels is an asset that's been created, accelerated and leveraged with the help of government incentives. The acceleration happened because increased demand was created through development of the tourism industry, and then asset leverage happened when additional competitors entered the market and helped spur innovation and growth.

The hotel sector is a good illustration of the strategic trajectory model. Hotels are built, demand is created through external (tourism, conferences and other attractions) and internal (design, unique attributes and shops) means, and the asset is leveraged as occupancy increases. The facilities need to be constantly monitored and evaluated, and reinvested (maintenance, upkeep, renovation), reinvented (expanded) or harvested (completely redone or rebuilt). Once there are dozens or hundreds of hotels going through this cycle in a developing market, the combined effects of the strategic vortex can be clearly seen.

Looking at these assets in the context of the strategic vortex of Dubai, it is easy to see how further acceleration and leverage are created by their interaction. The airport, Emirates and the tourism industry have grown in tandem, as part of the leadership's vision for Dubai. As one element grows, it allows and even encourages others to grow. The spillover effects create opportunities for investors in tourist attractions, restaurants and retailing. So as this part of the ecosystem develops, it creates leverage on a higher level that has contributed to the overall growth of the emirate and its economy.

Dubai Internet City and Dubai Media City

Sheikh Mohammed's analogy, likening Dubai Internet City to a virtual Dubai Creek, seems all the more apt when considering the asset leverage of the Technology, Electronic Commerce and Media Free Zone as a whole. The growth of cargo traffic in the Creek transformed Dubai. Similar growth in the free zone may have as great an influence on the economy of Dubai as the Creek once did.

The effects of asset acceleration in Dubai Internet City and Dubai Media City should be manifested in the asset leverage phase

– perhaps with fast growth as a result of increasing demand for office space or corporate synergies and networking opportunities, and innovation stemming from competition between companies. When Dubai Media City celebrated its second anniversary in January 2003, there was a great deal to be thankful for. The venture had grown far beyond expectations, having attracted over 620 companies by early 2003. After the initial building phase that created space for 96 companies in three buildings, two further phases have been completed, with more than 600,000 square feet of space in eight new buildings. The next phase of offices will be 'boutique' buildings, offering a campus of individual, highly customizable villas and a range of residential properties; educational and recreational facilities are also being developed.

Dubai Internet City and Dubai Media City have attracted companies large and small, and few of the major players in the technology and media industries are not represented. Compaq, Cisco, Microsoft, Oracle, Sun and Hewlett-Packard all have offices in Dubai Internet City. Sun Microsystems supports over 90 countries from this office, including all of Europe. Major players such as CNN, Reuters, Bertelsmann and several regional broadcasters are represented in Dubai Media City. In all, around 20 TV and radio broadcasters operate out of the city. Half of the companies in the zone are in marketing services or publishing, however, and many smaller providers supply the wide range of specialist services involved in print, broadcast and new-media production.

Asset leverage unleashes pent-up demand, as has happened in Dubai Internet City and Dubai Media City. Companies inside the zone should also benefit from synergies. Tejari.com has taken advantage of the range of services provided by other companies inside the two cities. One of the principal drivers of the company's success is its ability to find providers for training, value-added hosting services and any number of other services at arm's length. Tejari.com's Sheikha Lubna says that the growth of Dubai Internet City and Dubai Media City is largely organic, and she attributes this growth to the evolution of the network of companies and their interrelationships. These relationships are created and strengthened by a range of activities organized by the management of the two cities, such as regular breakfasts and networking events. One regular event in Dubai Media City is the Media *Majlis*, which, according to the city's website, provides 'an opportunity for partners to share ideas, suggestions and concerns with the senior management team of Dubai Media City'. It is 'great for networking too'.[5]

Microsoft works hard to cultivate a network of suppliers, and having many of them based in Dubai Internet City makes this much easier. The combination of large companies like Microsoft and smaller, more specialized providers helps to create a value network similar to the Silicon Valley model. The structure of the media production industry in Dubai Media City also encourages this, cultivating a diverse group of production, post-production and other creative services like those found in media districts in New York or London.

Dubai Media City has taken the idea of the small, specialized provider one step further by creating the Media Business Centre, which is home to 165 independent media workers with a wide variety of skills. Because employment law prevents self-employed foreigners from working in the UAE, the centre provides a unique opportunity for this group. It also gives companies within the free zone access to their talent. This is another example of leverage, with the demand for the services of these people acting as a spur to the innovative solution that allows them to work.

It is early days for innovation to emerge from competition among the companies operating in the Technology, Electronic Commerce and Media Free Zone. But Dubai Internet City and Dubai Media City have been leveraged beyond the zone in the strategic vortex of Dubai Inc. Their success has paved the way for further free zone developments focusing on industries as diverse as finance, healthcare and semiconductors. Their public relations value in the international business community adds to the image of

Dubai as fast-moving, progressive and technically savvy, paving the way for further growth.

Residential property

Another example of asset acceleration and leverage in Dubai is the market for residential property as a result of the initiative of developers and the enablement of the government. In 1999, new residential and mixed-use developments were announced that allowed foreigners to buy freehold or leasehold property along with an assurance of residency visas. Until that time, only nationals of the Gulf Co-operation Council countries[6] could buy property, and it was almost impossible to reside in the emirate if not employed. Laws and regulations in this area remain ambiguous, however, and the government of Dubai was still hard at work in early 2003 trying to clarify the intricacies of these new policies.

Any ambiguity regarding property ownership or visas does not seem to have had a detrimental effect on the market. The residential property boom began with the launch of the first phase of Emaar Property's Emirates Hills development. As the first development open to expatriates, take-up was fast and furious, with the initial phase selling out in hours. Demand increased further in May 2002, when the government announced that properties in selected developments would be available to buy freehold. This was at the time that the first houses and apartments became available on the Palm Jumeirah, prompting a sell-out in the first couple of days. Strong demand for properties continues, with buyers signing up on the spot the moment new developments are announced.

Ian Fairservice is founder and managing partner of Motivate Publishing. He emigrated to Dubai in the late 1970s and launched the local *What's On* magazine in 1979 (the Gulf's first English-language magazine) and now produces a range of magazines, books and custom publications covering the entire Gulf region. He was at the head of the queue when the Palm project was announced and bought a detached house on Palm Jumeirah. That same day, he made the decision to launch *Identity*, an interiors, design and property magazine aimed at property buyers like himself. The first issue appeared within four months, with features including the logistics and benefits of buying property and overviews of many of the developments on offer.

Ownership for foreigners is available only within certain developments. Emaar Properties has developed the majority of these projects, including Emirates Hills (villas), Arabian Ranches (villas and townhouses with golf and equestrian facilities) and Dubai Marina, a combination of different property types making up the largest such development in the world.[7] Emaar is a public company, listed on the Dubai Financial Market exchange, and the government owns almost one-third of its shares. In early 2003, Emaar had projects under various stages of development that would eventually be able to house 400,000 people.[8] That's almost enough to house nearly half of the current population of Dubai.[9]

Each Palm Island is also expected to have around 2,500 villas and 2,400 apartments for UAE nationals and foreigners to buy freehold. Residential properties ranging from studios to four-bedroom units are also available within the Technology, Electronic Commerce and Media Free Zone.

The growth in residential property and the relaxation of ownership restrictions will result in considerable economic and social change. By allowing anyone to buy property, the government is telling foreign investors that it wants not only their money but also themselves. Inevitably, services and related industries will grow to support this new group of permanent residents. Indeed, this is already happening as healthcare and educational institutions are developed.

All this will help attract families to Dubai and allow retired people to stay. The developers, meanwhile, are vigorously marketing the physical attractions of their developments together with the services included, ranging from pet sitting, landscaping and cleaning services to a residency visa with automatic renewal. Expatriate buyers who work in the free zones will recognize the convenience of the one-stop shop approach. However, some in Dubai believe that allowing foreigners to buy property puts UAE nationals at a disadvantage. A similar argument was used to oppose the free zones.

As you might expect, the government has a stake in each of the major property developments open to foreigners. The Palm Islands have also received a large amount of government financing, and the Jumeirah Beach Residence within the Technology, Electronic Commerce and Media Free Zone was built by Estithmar Realty, the government-owned developer of Dubai Internet City. Nevertheless, the government seems to be characteristically hands-off in its relations with the developers.

It remains to be seen whether any private developers will be allowed to offer their buyers residency visas along with their properties. In the meantime, it is clear that the government, through well-timed announcements of new developments, the staged introduction of the 99-year leasehold arrangement and the more recent freehold arrangement, has successfully leveraged its existing portfolio of residential property as there has been an explosive growth in demand. The danger is that supply may outstrip demand with the consequence that prices will go down, leaving some of those who purchase now looking at a loss. However, there is no sign that this is happening.

Counterpoint
The examples discussed in the chapter show how the effects of asset acceleration led to rapid growth and development. In each example, growth has happened organically after outside intervention helped to facilitate the acceleration effect. To illustrate what can happen when asset leverage is artificially stifled, we need look no further than some of the UAE's sponsorship, joint venture and agency laws and practices. Basically, if a foreign company or investor wishes to set up a business in Dubai, outside a free zone, he is required to have a local sponsoring partner who has a majority of

the equity. Originally, an effort by the government to invite foreign investment while creating the opportunity for UAE nationals to learn from the best.

Although the original aim was to also stimulate entrepreneurs, it can be argued that it has had the opposite effect. In practice, in many cases local partners appear to have little involvement in and little opportunity to learn from the partnership/joint venture. It seems that often there is a side agreement which specifies the true conditions and rights in the partnership/joint venture and that the local partner is in effect being paid a service fee to allow small or medium-size enterprises (SMEs) to establish themselves in Dubai.

In addition, and in contrast to the above, foreign companies that want to trade and sell their products and/or services in Dubai (outside a free zone) must have a local agent-distributor to represent them (there are some exceptions to this requirement, such as some professional services firms). These relationships, subject to whatever commercial agreements that may govern the relationship, may not be exclusive and may be terminated. For example, a large multinational could have a different agent – in effect a distributor – for each product line it sells, such as computers, televisions, etc. This gives some foreign companies more control over their products and services, and the local agent/distributor more incentive to perform because they know that they can be replaced.

In most cases agency practices seem to have worked well. Because a local agent/distributor knows and understands the local market – for example, where to locate a dealership and how to go about hiring and managing local staff – the risk to a multinational entering the market is reduced.

Overall, such sharing of activities has been an effective means of accelerating the internationalisation of trade in Dubai and the surrounding region. Many local agents/distributors have been active in their businesses, investing and expanding, and providing top-quality levels of service and a high degree of integration with, and sensitivity to, the local community. On the other hand some local joint venture sponsors appear to have taken their position for granted and put relatively little into the businesses they are involved in as sponsors. However, 'sleeping' or 'silent' partners may now find themselves expected to do more than they have been doing or they may find their joint venture or agency being taken away from them and given to someone else.

The agency and sponsorship practices that Dubai has adopted are common throughout much of the Gulf region. However, it is important to realize some of their shortcomings, particularly of the need to have a majority local joint venture partner. SMEs, the foundation of much economic growth, may have been held back by these requirements, which raise the cost and increase the complexity of doing business in Dubai and thereby deter investors from entering the market.

At the same time, many question the usefulness of the majority shareholder requirement now that competition is thriving within the free zones, albeit not for trade in the local market. If the regulation was to be relaxed, it could open the market to yet more competition, but it could also remove one of the biggest incentives for companies to locate in the free zones – although the one-stop shop advantage would remain. Thus, as rules and regulations evolve, Dubai must achieve a balance that allows it to create greater economic growth and prosperity for its people.

Conclusion

This chapter has shown how the effects of asset acceleration can lead to asset leverage on many levels, given empowering leadership with a good sense of timing that isn't afraid to step back and adopt a hands-off approach. Asset leverage can mean rapid growth innovation, competition and collaboration among players involved in the strategic vortex.

As happened in the hotel industry, the Technology, Electronic Commerce and Media Free Zone and the residential property market, the resulting growth and innovation can be dramatic. But, as in the case of stifling sponsorship practices, complacency and suboptimization can result if asset acceleration is not allowed to move on to its logical next step.

Asset leverage can create significant value within groups of assets or within the strategic vortex as a whole. In order to manage this optimally, leadership has to keep an eye on things and take action when required.

Notes

1 Related by Anis Al Jallaf of the Dubai International Financial Centre

2 Extracted from http://dubaitourism.co.ae

3 Although the Jin Mao Building in Shanghai is taller, it is composed of hotel and office space (from www.skyscrapers.com)

4 www.emiratesbank.com, www.khaleejtimes.co.ae

5 www.dubaimediacity.com

6 The Co-operation Council for the Arab States of the Gulf (GCC) is a regional organisation formed in 1981, consisting of Bahrain, Kuwait, Oman, Qatar, Saudi Arabia and the United Arab Emirates

7 www.emaar.com/marina/about/

8 Scott, B. 2002. 'The benefits of buying', Identity, Issue 1, November/December

9 2001 total population (UAE nationals and resident expatriates) totalled 910,300

8 Closing the loop

*Falling is fine, as long you fall forward, and when you get up you are
ahead of where you were …*

LAURA TYSON in discussion with SHEIKH MOHAMMED

We have seen how assets in Dubai have been created, accelerated and
leveraged to form the basis for the growth that the emirate has experienced in recent years. As we've implied, this process is by no means
linear, with a set beginning and end. It's cyclical, with the strategic
vortex growing exponentially as a result of interactions between
individual assets and groups of assets. The asset leverage stage, as
we've seen, is where much of the inherent value of an asset can be
unleashed, with little outside intervention required at that point.
But this growth can continue only for so long before it needs some
attention. When that point is reached, how should you proceed?

There are three options available to decision-makers once an
asset stops developing optimally: reinvestment, reinvention and
harvesting. Brief explanations of each of these options follow.

At its most fundamental level, asset reinvestment involves maintenance, upkeep and further development of an existing asset or
group of similar assets. When the data indicate that an asset is
being fully and efficiently utilized, it will need maintenance to keep
it functioning properly. Often, additional resources will need to be
allocated to ensure that the asset is able to change to meet growing
or changing demands on it.

In the context of the strategic vortex, this step is crucial for estab-

Strategic trajectory

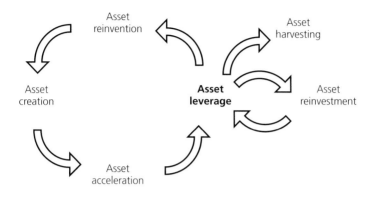

lishing an ever-developing core to which future assets can be added and grown. Both infrastructural assets and revenue-generating assets need to be developed to ensure that the integrity of the strategic vortex is maintained and strengthened to allow for future growth and increases in momentum.

Asset reinvention is the second option. After experiencing the growth of asset leverage, it may be that additional uses for an asset have emerged, or that the main utility of the asset has been exhausted, but another use presents itself. So when it's clear that an asset can be used in a different or additional way, it's time to consider reinventing that asset. This ultimately leads back to the asset creation phase for the strategic trajectory cycle to start all over again. Then, whether the asset starts with a new use, or carries on as before with a new spin-off, reinvention integrates accumulated learning to add exponential amounts of value to the strategic vortex as it begins again.

The third option is asset harvesting. When an asset has no further useful life, it should be retired to avoid becoming a liability to the system. Its resources can then be redeployed to support new or existing assets, set aside for future use, or disposed of entirely.

Success factors

Effective decision-making depends on having the information necessary for a decision to be made and there being appropriate and well-oiled channels to ensure the decision is communicated. In Dubai, commonly accepted project appraisal techniques are often used to provide the information that the decision-makers need. For example, the Palm Island development was the subject of reams of studies by numerous individual consulting firms before it went ahead; in fact, the government of Dubai appears to have enlisted the help of every major management consulting firm in recent years. Although a project like the Burj Al Arab would be unlikely to satisfy any publicly traded company's project assessment criteria, it made sense for the government to invest in it because of the buzz it would create and the boost it would give to Dubai's unique image and, in turn, the tourism industry. As the unwillingness of the merchant community to develop the Dubai Marina showed, if Dubai is to drive towards its own ambitious vision, the government has to decide the criteria for major asset creation. In short, strong leadership and vision is at the heart of successful decision-making in the emirate.

Accessibility and visibility

The accessibility of Sheikh Mohammed is a key factor that allows two-way communication and keeps his office abreast of everything that's happening in Dubai. The more structured forum for consultations with the rulers, the *majlis*, is another important mechanism.

Dubai Media City's Abdulhamid Juma describes how Sheikh Mohammed goes out of his way to learn about the needs and concerns of the people and local businesses:

> Two days ago, he was in the old city. He talked with every store owner there. It took three and a half hours. You see him at an exhibition, he doesn't come just to be seen there, he really talks to

people. He understands them. And if he wants to know more, he invites companies to come to him with presentations on what they do. He's very much involved.

As Sheikha Lubna says, 'Sheikh Mohammed is accessible. The problem with a lot of CEOs is that they aren't.' Thus she reinforces the often-used metaphor of Sheikh Mohammed being the man running 'Dubai Inc'.

The accessibility and visibility of Sheikh Mohammed also makes a significant contribution to the trust that individuals and businesses have in him and his office. By having lunch with few attendants in bustling public restaurants and strolling on his own through shopping arcades, he at once communicates that he is aware of what happens in daily life in Dubai and that he is part of it.

Such openness demonstrates national and civic pride, as Microsoft's Abdullatif Al Mulla explains:

> The royal families always leave their doors open for any ideas, any opinions, as an opportunity for people to exhibit their good will for the country.

There is similar accessibility to senior management in government departments as well as in private companies. Khalid Bin Sulayem of the Department of Trade and Commerce Marketing explains how this happens:

> Any employee can come at any time and meet with me or call me. Not only in working hours, even in evenings at home. Every day people do this. After I have dinner at home people come. Even until midnight or one o'clock in the morning.

Raja Easa Al Gurg echoes this statement in the context of her large family-owned company, the Easa Saleh Al Gurg Group:

I believe that an open-door policy is a very important thing. It makes people feel that they are working from their heart, that this is *their* business and they want to improve it.

So when decisions need to be made, these managers clearly have more to work with than their weekly reports and dashboards.

Accessibility and visibility are important, then, not only for their practical application – conveying individual concerns, opinions and options to the decision-makers – but also because they instil confidence and a sense of self-worth and value in others.

Management by majlis

A close, almost symbiotic relationship between the business community and the government works in several ways. Shehab Gargash describes the co-dependence of these two groups:

The business community cannot live without government, and the government cannot live without the business community – both of them recognize this. It's a very flat society, so the distance between the bottom and the top is very small. Word gets to the ruler or the crown prince very fast through his own team of department heads within the government or through the business community. He also holds a lot of meetings throughout the year with various groups.

Many of these meetings are held in what is commonly known as a *majlis*. The *majlis* is an Arab tradition, usually involving a community leader gathering a group to address people's concerns, hear ideas, communicate plans, or simply as a social forum to gather friends and family. It can take many forms.

In Sheikh Rashid's time, his *majlis* consisted of a set group of leaders which functioned in place of a formal government organization. More recently, the term has taken on a broader meaning in Dubai, ranging from the informal sessions at which virtually anyone is welcome to exclusive meetings among senior government officials and/or business leaders.

Many business and community leaders have a *majlis*, and many homes have a room or area dedicated to hosting these sessions. At any *majlis*, guests discuss current events and business, watch television (invariably programmes on news or current affairs), have tea and sweets, and make deals. The enduring popularity of this phenomenon guarantees that news travels fast from one *majlis* to the next, eventually reaching Sheikh Mohammed's *majlis*, where the most important strategic decisions regarding the emirate are often made.

Ahmed Al Banna, deputy director general, studies and international affairs, at the Dubai Chamber of Commerce and Industry, explains:

> Let's say I have a problem I know cannot be sorted out. I know that Sheikh Mohammed will be in his *majlis* for lunch around one o'clock. I go and explain the issue to him, and he gives me his feedback. I have lunch with him and I leave. That's what happens with all government departments, all the leadership.

Abdulhamid Juma elaborates:

> The *majlis* closes the gap between him and his CEOs and managers. He said to all the directors general, 'If you have an idea, you come straight to me.' He loves ideas. 'I know your boss, I see him every day. I want to see *you* once in a while.'

Sheikh Mohammed's *majlis* isn't only for ideas and problem-solving, nor is it only for UAE nationals. Raja Trad, a Lebanese advertising executive, explains:

> Sheikh Mohammed's office will pick up representatives from each industry, and they will call us into the *majlis*. We'll be around 100

people and Sheikh Mohammed will say, 'No taboos. You represent Dubai. Dubai is not just for the nationals, Dubai is for you. You contributed to the success of Dubai.' And then he will invite people to stand up and talk about anything.

Both good news and bad news are conveyed in the *majlis*. This helps problems to be addressed as soon as they arise. In the rulers' *majlis*, the rulers learn what's important to the community, and the members of the community learn the rulers' perspective, as well as those of their peers. Key people come together, pool their knowledge and come up with solutions that they will all endorse.

So the *majlis* provides a forum for socializing, problem-solving and debate at many levels of the community. It's also a means for communication in every direction among stakeholder groups, extending right up to the rulers, who are known to ring senior officials during the *majlis* to draw their attention to issues that have been raised and to get them to take action.

Management wearing many hats

Another way in which the government and the business community work together is by combining leadership roles in a way that rarely happens in the West. Senior government officials head a variety of public, private, semi-private and independently managed government-owned companies. This ensures a mutuality in the interests of business and government. Members of the inner circle of leaders who are involved in many private and governmental organizations are thus in a position to feed information back to the rulers on practically any subject. In effect, they appear to take the place of governance boards or consultative bodies.

The system is based on a sort of government patronage, which has to be benign and intelligent if it is to work to the advantage of the emirate as a whole. Abdullatif Al Mulla explains:

They choose the best people, the people that can be trusted, the people who can contribute without looking forward for a return – eventually they get rewarded, but this is not their first consideration. Not everyone is looking for financial compensation, some are looking for recognition not only in Dubai or the United Arab Emirates, but also across the region. If anybody has a very successful initiative, he will become well known in the Arab region.

The range of high-ranking jobs someone may hold is illustrated in the following examples:

□ Anis Al Jallaf is CEO and managing director of Emirates Bank International; and chairman of the Dubai International Financial Centre.
□ Mohammed Ali Alabbar is director general of the Department of Economic Development; chairman of Emaar; vice-chairman of Dubai Aluminium Company, Dubai World Trade Centre and Dubai Cable Company; and a director of National Bank of Dubai and the Dubai Chamber of Commerce and Industry.
□ Sultan Bin Sulayem is executive chairman of the Ports, Customs and Free Zone Corporation; and chairman of Dubai Palm Developers and Tejari.com.

When asked how he manages to do so many demanding jobs, Sultan Bin Sulayem explains simply that he likes it, and that he gets bored when not working. He also says that he goes out of his way to communicate with all the people under him, with a regular pro-gramme of training schemes and management feedback sessions.

The multiple roles of many of these figures also come from a long-standing Arab tradition: when someone succeeds, he – or, increasingly frequently, she – is rewarded with more responsibility. Sheikha Lubna was part of Sultan Bin Sulayem's team at Jebel Ali port before being asked to head the e-government initiative and then, soon after, to start up Tejari.com.

But some question what's often called the 'Superman syndrome'. They believe that some high-ranking government officials remain in their positions too long, with the result that their effectiveness may decrease and that they may become less good at adapting to changes in the evolving business environment. However, in view of the pace of change and the constant need to adapt, there appears to be little room for laggards and the system does appear to have created natural efficiencies.

Other conduits

As Dubai grows, there is always a danger of the government becoming bigger and more bureaucratic. But Sheikh Mohammed's distaste for new layers of government suggests this will not happen. Anita Mehra Homayoun of the Department of Civil Aviation describes the importance of maintaining the traditional practices:

> As Dubai gets bigger and bigger, and the number of merchants gets bigger and bigger, the government losing touch becomes a danger. Then we'd become like many Western democracies. In Sheikh Rashid's days, someone would come to the *majlis* and say 'I've lost five camels', and the Ruler would give him replacements. Things are different now, but the same kind of thing happens on a larger scale.

To ensure that the government is able to keep up with people's needs, decidedly modern initiatives have been developed. One is the e-government portal launched in 2002. The objective of the portal is to facilitate interaction between the government, the public and the business community and to contribute to turning Dubai into a leading economic centre. By 2003, 600 services were available, involved in providing information and assisting transactions in such areas as business, health, education, housing, law and the judicial system, and tourism. Users can pay fines, apply for and renew a variety of licences and permits, and find out about a wide range of government services.

According to Sheikha Lubna, whom Sheikh Mohammed trusted with developing and launching the portal:

> He wanted more transparency in the government itself. He wanted to demonstrate the government being customer-centric.

This transparency should allow more accurate and more timely information to be available, as Abdulhamid Juma says:

> If Sheikh Mohammed wants to sit at home or in his office and know how many visas were issued on that day, that information should be on the portal.

As it grows, the portal should be able to provide a valuable amount of quantitative data that will aid effective decision-making.

Another means for Dubai's leaders to learn about what's going on in government departments is the Dubai Government Excellence Programme, which is run by a private company and was established to improve efficiency and innovation in government. Government divisions, departments, teams and initiatives are ranked according to a comprehensive framework, including financial performance. Feedback from 'mystery shoppers', who approach government departments in a variety of guises, is also incorporated into the assessment criteria.

Results of the rankings are made public and those whose performance is relatively poor are made aware that they must improve. This programme is crucial in creating government transparency and also provides an incentive for every part of government to perform well. The extensive data-gathering and analysis involved in the programme provides further information for the government to use in its decision-making process. It also provides opportunities for benchmarking and learning across the government. One government official explained:

> The government has implemented the quality programmes so that

departments will learn from one another and improve. This has improved our customer service by a tremendous amount.

Some of the programme's methods have been adopted by Sheikh Mohammed's office, which now sends mystery shoppers independently to different parts of the government. One official told of an excitable character who turned up at his office looking for a job, and who was suspected of being a plant from The Executive Office. The official later discovered that this was not the case, but awareness of the possibility exists throughout the civil service.

Still room for improvement

There is no shortage of information available to the government, but it has been suggested that the accuracy and timeliness of some data need to be improved, which may prove to be an increasingly important issue as the emirate develops. Sheikh Mohammed referred to the 50 weather stations around Dubai that provide real-time data, and said that he would like to see business information with the same immediacy. The data exist but aren't always shared between departments let alone available electronically in real time.

As Anita Mehra Homayoun indicated, a major challenge for Dubai will be maintaining the close contact between the ruler and the community. Better information and better information flows will help do this and will also maintain the effectiveness of the decision-making process.

Options in practice

Asset reinvestment

Examples of asset reinvestment are rife in Dubai, as many of the infrastructural assets and other large core assets were created in their initial form decades ago and have had to develop to sustain the pace of growth.

The road network is constantly under construction, particularly outside the old town centre where new roads are being built. The mushroom-like construction of office and apartment buildings along Sheikh Zayed Road causes tremendous traffic congestion at many times during a typical day. The layout of the road means that it can take over half an hour to get from a building on one side of the divided road to one immediately opposite.

The pace at which the roads are being built is startling, even for Dubai's residents. Everyone seems to have a story to tell about getting lost because the road layout has changed. One man who went on a short business trip returned to find that the airport lot where he'd left his car only a few days before had been moved to make way for more building. His car was safe and sound in another lot.

At the start of 2003, a $109 million programme was under way to upgrade the road network in Dubai, including a new bridge over the Creek.

By 2008, the new Dubai Railway should be complete, consisting of two lines, 37 stations and over 50 kilometres of track. The need for the new railway may not be immediately apparent, but there is a large group of foreign residents on modest incomes who will greatly benefit from such a system as an addition to the already stretched public transport network. Tourists will also benefit from the railway, which should help to alleviate the growing congestion on Dubai's roads and motorways.

Further major initiatives to expand the capacity of both electricity generation and water provision were undertaken early in the 21st century to meet the rapidly growing demand. As roads, offices and residences threaten to overwhelm the city, the development of several parks and green spaces is also under way, including expansion of Dubai Zoo, which is moving to a new site.

This isn't being done just to maintain the status quo, however; there's a strong competitive element to asset reinvestment as well. The ports, airport and Emirates have also undergone frequent expansion over the years, each helping to fuel the growth of tourism and make life and business more comfortable in the emirate. The combined effect of these assets within the strategic vortex is important, even if they are merely being grown and expanded over time.

Abdullatif Al Mulla explains how he sees asset reinvestment working in Dubai:

> It's important to continually update your operations. The government of Dubai recognizes this and takes risks to keep improving. This is why Dubai is one of the only places in the world where the public sector moves faster than the private sector.

This is consistent with the government's vision, which involves the creation of superlative assets at high speed.

In the hotel industry, standards are being raised constantly by new entrants with increasingly spectacular offerings. This forces existing hotels to implement renovation programmes and continue to improve in order to stay competitive. The retail sector has seen similar growth in recent years, but, as ever more spectacular shopping venues are created with built-in entertainment and restaurants, the older malls look tired and can start to become less popular. Much the same is true in the commercial property market. As the city has expanded beyond the centre, better and better office buildings have become available. The World Trade Centre was once on the outskirts of the town and a highly prestigious address; now it is the first of many newer high rise towers, not the least of which is Emirates Towers virtually next door. Several of the buildings in the same area along Sheikh Zayed Road are beginning to seem slightly downmarket compared with some of their newer neighbours, even though almost none of them is more than a decade old. And an increasing number of businesses are moving from their existing office space to offices in Dubai Internet City and Dubai Media City, forcing some buildings to undergo refurbishment just to stay in the game. Hence the need for continuous investment so that hotels, shopping centres, commercial and residential buildings stay ahead of the game or at least keep up with the fast pace of change. This is already happening in many of the earlier developments mentioned above.

In many cases, such as the facilities in Dubai's ports, international competition drives reinvestment. Sultan Bin Sulayem describes the constant upgrading of Jebel Ali Port to keep up with Singapore.

> Whatever you see in Singapore, you see here. Sometimes we are more advanced than them, sometimes they are more advanced than us. We invest in different things. For example, Singapore invested in a single crane that carries two containers. We decided to get a faster, more advanced crane that worked better and was less expensive. Later, they came to see ours and decided to change. Sometimes we are better, sometimes they are better, but we are very, very close.

Asset reinvention

Asset reinvention can involve repositioning an asset that has outlived its original purpose, although it is early days for this to have happened in Dubai. It can be like brand extension: developing a new use for an existing asset. There are many examples of this in the emirate.

The Dubai Police Academy was set up by Sheikh Rashid in 1968 to help train local people to supplement the Trucial Oman Scouts, a regional force funded and armed by the British.[1] Since that time, the academy has been reinvented many times, taking on its present form in 1987 and becoming independent in 1998. Over the years, it has retained its affiliation with the Police Department, but has reinvented itself as a institute for higher learning, offering a variety of law degrees and evening programmes in addition to its cadet training. The academy is also now recognized as a centre for excellence in the region, accepting recruits from other Gulf Co-operation Council countries. Women are also eligible to take part in academy programmes, including a combination of police sciences and military training.[2]

The Dubai Ports Authority has pursued a similar model, having developed such an expertise in port and free zone management that it could begin to apply them in other countries. The newly formed Dubai Ports International more than doubled productivity in the first three years of a 20-year contract it signed in 1999 to manage and operate Jeddah's container terminal with a local partner. The following year, it invested in Djibouti's port, this time doubling productivity in the first year of managing its operations.

The Dubai Shopping Festival is another asset that has undergone multiple reinventions. Inspired by the Great Singapore Sale, it was started in 1996 to create an attraction for visitors from around the region and stimulate retail trade. By 2002, the shopping festival was attracting 2.7 million visitors, and more than $1 billion was spent.[3] Hotels, transport, shops and restaurants all benefit from the event; some earn more during the festival than during the rest of the year.

The Global Village is a reinvention spin-off from the Dubai Shopping Festival. It began as six pavilions representing different countries on a plot next to the Creek for the duration of the festival. By 2002, there were 32 pavilions from all over the world, offering shopping, entertainment and food. The Global Village has proven to be such a success that it will operate throughout the year from 2006. The Dubai Summer Surprise is a reinvented Dubai Shopping Festival in the heat of the summer, focusing on family activities for the regional market, with a different theme each year. The Dubai World Cup horse race used to coincide with the shopping festival, taking advantage of the influx of visitors. However, in 2003 the race took place afterwards because the shopping festival was moved to take advantage of school and religious holidays. All the indications are that the race is well able to stand up on its own.

One example of reinvention is at the personal level. Dubai International Airport was one of the first airports in the world to implement an electronic pass system called e-gate. This allows registered users to bypass immigration and enter the country with just their e-card and a fingerprint scan. The programme is open to all UAE residents, as well as citizens of 34 countries that are eligible for on-the-spot visas. The programme has had a remarkably fast take-up, with 3,500 citizens from 45 countries signing up in the first month. When an immigration attendant was asked if such technologies made him fear for his job, he replied that if this job disappeared, he was confident that he would be given a new job. This speaks volumes about the mindset of people in Dubai. This man had complete trust in the government and his employer to do right by him. This belief, in turn, gave him the confidence to do his job well and indeed convinced one of the authors to get an e-gate card.

In each of the examples of asset reinvention described above, changes were made with careful consideration, based on the best information available and guided by the asset's place in the vision of Dubai. In terms of the strategic vortex model, spin-off assets start the cycle anew at the asset creation stage, while upgraded assets remain in asset leverage, still growing and interacting with other elements.

Asset harvesting

One example of asset harvesting in Dubai was created in the Technology, Electronic Commerce and Media Free Zone at the same time as Dubai Internet City. The Dubai Ideas Oasis, a dotcom incubator, was a short-lived initiative, and it seems to have been easily forgotten in the light of the successes of Dubai Internet City and Dubai Media City. The government provided seed funds, but further venture capital didn't emerge. But in the end, according to one of those interviewed for this book, there just weren't enough good ideas to sustain the project. The Dubai Ideas Oasis was put on hold indefinitely, although several of the original start-ups that participated are continuing to manage their businesses in Dubai Internet City. The facilities and resources of the Dubai Ideas Oasis have since been taken over and put to use there.

There will be many candidates for asset harvesting if the agency laws are changed. As already discussed, these laws provide the prominent trading families with monopolies in many areas, thus in some cases preventing competition and asset leverage, though it is clear that some monopoly businesses are very well managed and customer focused, reinvesting regularly to keep up with changing market requirements and to take advantage of new opportunities. It is unclear whether such changes may happen in the foreseeable future and what the effects would be. But as the economy grows and attracts more skilled workers with disposable income, it is reasonable to expect that the demand for luxury cars, for example, will also grow. Either the existing sole sellers of each brand will reap the benefits, or, if competition is allowed, the benefits may be shared and buyers may also enjoy lower prices. If this happens, the incumbents may continue to prosper, but some may be unable to compete and may have to harvest some of the assets that currently seem so prosperous. Asset harvesting should not be equated with failure; some projects simply have a limited useful life and must at some point be retired. Nevertheless, there is an aversion to failure in Dubai that may help to explain why few projects seem to have reached this stage. Abdulhamid Juma puts it succinctly:

We don't have projects fail here. If it's going to fail, we'll change it.

The pride that many people feel in their work is a strong disincentive to perceived failure. Even in the face of extreme risk, failure is never considered to be an option by some, as Sultan Bin Sulayem says:

Even if a project is barely able to be done, there are people who will never accept failure. If they fail, it will be a big embarrassment. I would be very embarrassed if the Palm didn't work, even though the risk of failure is very high. They manage, and they do it. This is what we try to promote.

He is a good example of a senior executive who stays involved with his projects at every level, making adjustments and changes whenever needed so that they never approach the point of failure.

This perspective is shared by many business leaders in the West, particularly successful entrepreneurs who aren't shy about reallocating resources when signs of failure begin to loom. As development in Dubai continues, it is inevitable that there will be failures; accepting this fact may prove a challenge for government and business community alike.

Managing the portfolio

The strategic vortex model is a fluid one, and can be applied at several different levels. An asset can be a company, an organization, a facility or a bundle of related entities. When you put multiple assets together and manage the portfolio strategically, you begin to see radical growth on a large scale. This is what has occurred in Dubai.

Initial assets were created to build on existing strengths: the Creek was developed and ports were built. To supplement the flow of goods in and out, industrial free zones for businesses to set up operations were created. Then, anticipating increased demand for air passenger and freight traffic, Emirates Airline was created. The airport was expanded and the Airport Free Zone was created to supplement the existing free zones. To diversify the economy into high-value-added knowledge-based industries, the Technology, Electronic Commerce and Media Free Zone was created. The influx of companies and workers led to a demand for world-class facilities such as education, healthcare and housing. Most recently, the Dubai International Financial Centre was conceived with the intention of making the emirate an internationally recognized institutional finance hub and a gateway in the region for capital markets and investment. Throughout this process the infrastructure has been built and upgraded to support the needs of the growing system, although it has occasionally fallen behind, as the level of traffic congestion makes all too clear.

Each new asset has taken advantage of the business ecosystem into which it has been introduced. For example, the development of Port Rashid benefited from Dubai's existing reputation as a trading port, and the Technology, Electronic Commerce and Media Free Zone was developed as a result of knowledge and experience from Jebel Ali. The Dubai International Financial Centre is the next natural step, albeit a large and risky one. If it's successful, this will in large part be thanks to the size and momentum of the asset base that's already been established. Essa Abdulfattah Kazim, director general of the Dubai Financial Market, describes the market readiness for the financial centre:

> We have the critical mass now. We can capitalize on the name of Dubai. If you ask anyone in finance today where the centre for finance is in the region, he would say it is Bahrain. But because of the reputation of Dubai, we believe that this is the right time for developing the Dubai International Financial Centre and the financial sector here.

This sort of strategic thinking and decisive action can only be possible when leaders are well informed and surrounded by like-minded staff who are in touch with a wide range of stakeholders. With this sort of group at the helm, the right assets can be created at just the right time, and their growth can be managed optimally within the ecosystem. As we've seen, initial assets require bold, risky moves – think of Sheikh Rashid's early initiatives or, more recently, the Palm Islands – so they need to be chosen with care. They will form the foundation on which other assets will grow and develop. They'll need to be solid and scaleable like Emirates Airline, the airport and the ports and free zones have been. (If it seems easy, think of the problems many other airports have had in expanding to meet demand over recent years.) Unless these assets are the right ones, created in the right way, they won't be able to support the momentum of assets that are added later.

Once you've got these assets right, though, additional assets should present decreased risk because of the momentum already built up, and because you're building on existing assets and knowledge. This is why it's important for leadership to be able to step back and regard the ecosystem as a whole, as well as the detailed components that interact within it. A winning strategy, then, is able to leverage past successes (and what you have learnt from failures) to determine which assets to create and when, so that they have an optimal effect on the rest of the system. The principal factor is being able to understand what the ecosystem wants and needs, based on external factors (the economy, markets, customers, competitors) and internal factors (other assets, available resources), and then put the strategy into action rapidly.

Notes

1 Wilson, *Father of Dubai*
2 www.dubaipolice.gov.ae
3 Dubai Shopping Festival press release, 13 February 2003

9 Corporate implications

The speed of the boss is the speed of the team.

LEE IACOCCA, former Chrysler chairman

In the dramatic transformation of Dubai many themes stand out – strategy, vision and leadership – all of which are commonly covered in business books. But it isn't often that they are associated in business with governments. It is the innovative application of these themes in Dubai that makes it such an interesting example, from which can be drawn a range of lessons for use in today's corporations and other organizations.

This book has sought to explore the fundamental issue of how organizations can achieve large-scale, rapid growth. Expanding current business operations through the extension of existing products or services or entering new markets is one way. Others include mergers and acquisitions, attempts to innovate outside the current product-market offerings and reorganizing around 'skunk-works' project teams.[1] But each of these methods has potential shortcomings.

Over half of mergers and acquisitions fail because they don't achieve the much-trumpeted synergies they were supposed to, or because of culture clashes or a host of other reasons. The failure is all the more painful when the acquisition was made at a price that included a high premium. The problem with skunk-works is that it invariably takes longer than expected to produce results.

As is the case with many if not most corporations, Dubai was not blessed with abundant resources when its rapid development began in the mid-20th century, so its rulers had little choice but to build on their existing strengths. This is what Sheikh Rashid did, beginning with the development of the Dubai Creek and building the airport back in the early 1960s, adding to the region's value as a port and a hub. With these small steps he set Dubai on a path that has led the emirate to where it is today, with a lot of care, attention and adjustment on the way as well as enormous drive.

This chapter considers how Dubai succeeded in order to draw lessons that can be applied across a wide range of organizations. Four broad themes are covered: active, creative leadership; the asset creation, acceleration and leverage stages of the strategic vortex model; the strategic vortex model itself; and some of the principal considerations in managing a portfolio of assets to enable rapid growth.

Active leadership

One of the crucial components of a successful strategy is active leadership. Dubai has proved this through its own distinctive style of active leadership, which fosters innovation, breaks through boundaries, involves taking risks and instils confidence among stakeholders – in stark contrast to many business and government leaders today and in the past.

Active leadership is important at every stage of the strategic trajectory model. There will almost always be multiple assets in their own strategic trajectories interacting within the larger ecosystem. While one asset is being created another may be being accelerated and yet another being harvested, and so the leadership characteristics required at each phase need to be demonstrated.

Set the vision

Vision is frequently cited as an important element of leadership. Indeed, the authors' experience in Dubai reinforces this view. But vision in Dubai is more than just an expression of where it is meant to be going. It also has a multidimensional, cascading effect, providing inspiration and goals for managers and civil servants alike as they consider what the vision means to them and their own domain within greater Dubai Inc.

Just over half a century ago Dubai was little more than sand. The cornerstone of its economy, pearl diving, had been decimated. Out of this adversity, the vision to create a major economic centre was born. Much of the ensuing development has occurred in the last 25 or so years, but the vision of stretching to new levels is seen in all aspects of Dubai – its airport, seaports, real estate and other developments – and its facilities are virtually without parallel.

Part of the strength of the Dubai vision is its flexibility. Everyone seems to have a different idea of exactly what the vision is, so the leadership has succeeded not only in creating a widespread understanding of the emirate's priorities, direction and values, but also in encouraging a climate in which different stakeholders can create their own impression of the vision and determine how best to achieve it. This flexible type of vision is more effective than a static vision statement, reproduced in corporate literature and promptly ignored or forgotten until the next internal strategic realignment.

The Dubai vision is a living vision, one that has as many meanings as there are stakeholders. It can only be accurately expressed as the sum of all of its constituents' visions, but that nevertheless serves as a set of guiding principles for all activities. It does incorporate quantifiable targets – for example, so many tourists by 2010 and so many airline departures by 2030 – but these figures serve to add depth to the greater vision of Dubai becoming a leading hub for visitors and businesses, with all the amenities and the high standard of living that go with this.

It is an all-encompassing vision that guides all stages of the cycle of asset creation, acceleration and leverage. The first step is for the leadership to decide on its vision, which must be one that can be understood, interpreted and applied at every level of the organization, but must also have a depth that conveys the true meaning of the intended messages. Once the vision has been set, the most effective way for the leadership to communicate and reinforce it is by example.

Lead by example

The government in Dubai takes tremendous risks by investing in infrastructure and commercial development projects which in most cases no private business would consider, but which private investors invariably follow. It appears to be reasonably transparent and intolerant of corruption. Government departments are customer-oriented, striving to provide truly excellent service. The government is constantly seen to be striving for the best in everything it does, all seemingly focused on the realization of the Dubai vision.

It also presents a consistent message, constantly reinforced by its actions and by self-examination through programmes such as the Dubai Award for Government Excellence. By holding up high-performing government departments as exemplars as well as reporting on those whose standards of performance need improvement, the government shows its commitment to high standards and, at the same time, sends a strong message about the standards it expects from the private sector.

For a vision to be achieved it must be supported by active leadership. Seeing your leader working harder than you do is bound to be inspiring. Government leaders in Dubai talk enthusiastically about their 'open-door policies' and their habit of seeing workers until late in the evening, and it is clear that the same practices are catching on among managers of private companies.

Leadership by example is a simple concept that can be easily adopted in any organization. When leaders constantly strive to embody the organizational vision, it is much easier for others to follow.

Instil confidence

Another important element of Dubai's leadership is the ability to instil confidence. Many huge projects, most recently the Palm Islands, involved daunting deadlines on top of already ambitious objectives. But in each case, the project managers describe how Sheikh Mohammed gave them the confidence to get the job done. In turn, that confidence was passed on to members of their teams.

Clearly this is partly due to the leadership's ability to provide latitude to get the job done and the understanding that the necessary resources and support will be provided. By setting ambitious goals and ensuring that the resources are in place to achieve them, Dubai's rulers have created what Sheikha Lubna calls 'an army of leaders', all taking responsibility for building Dubai and achieving the vision.

Showing confidence in managers and building their confidence is an important leadership role in any organization. If leaders communicate and live the vision, and then enable others to take part in achieving it, everyone will gain confidence in themselves and the enterprise, reinforcing the vision in the process.

Manage through trust

The morality of the traditional trading culture of Dubai combined with the governmental structure has created a society in which, to a significant degree, trust takes the place of formal rules or regulation. Just as gold traders on the Creek took each other at their word, many of the freedoms enjoyed in the current business environment exist because of a sense of trust between business and the government. Instead of issuing regulations that impinge on everyone, Dubai's government prefers to focus on detecting the small number of wrongdoers and excluding them. But it is accepted that regulation may be necessary in some circumstances to create trust and confidence in the system as, for example, in financial services.

In the West there has been a shift towards a regulatory approach and a reliance on legal mechanisms such as highly detailed contracts to govern business relationships. The practical lesson from Dubai is that governments and firms alike would do well to strip out unnecessary regulations, restrictions, red tape and procedures, and to put more emphasis on building a value system founded on trust. This will, as it does in Dubai, allow greater flexibility, encourage more effective communication and teamwork, and enable faster adjustment to change. It may not be easy to do, but it is surely worth a try.

Be visible and accessible

Another element of effective leadership is visibility, being seen as an ever-present part of the system. Sheikh Mohammed is always out and about in Dubai, mixing with his people in restaurants or in the mall, or driving around on his own. He also pays attention to detail, as any good CEO would. He is frequently seen checking on the progress of projects or meeting local workers. Despite his position, he is an active and visible part of Dubai Inc. Contrast this with many of the Western CEOs who have recently departed, who seemed more concerned with stock options than with building a business. Today, people are too well educated and well informed to be led by passive, hollow vision statements. The CEO must be visible to the entire organization as being an active agent of change, not an invisible demigod espousing an unattainable ideal.

Related to this is how a leader can learn from people at all levels, not just a few elite workers or influential figures. This comes down to accessibility. Dubai's open-door policy enables business people to meet Sheikh Mohammed and express their thoughts about the implications of new government initiatives on their business.

Many corporations have open-door policies, but few work like this. Instead of examining and resolving problems, they are referred and disappear into a bureaucratic black hole. With some open-door policies, the door is one that leads to diminishing career prospects as those who raise an issue find themselves ostracized, sidelined or excluded. Sheikh Mohammed recognizes that the success of this policy is ensuring that those who confide in him won't be punished for their opinions; he regards it as an opening into a world of information and insights too valuable to risk. Without the perceived safety of this process of information sharing, only yes-men would get through, sacrificing the real-time value and losing many opportunities to improve. When managing large projects that are proceeding quickly, failure to get accurate, rapid feedback can spell disaster.

This technique isn't limited to Sheikh Mohammed's office. Other senior government officials and managers in the private sector embrace an open-door policy as well. One interviewed by the authors said that it is known among his staff that any negative repercussions involving people who come to him will be dealt with severely, but this hardly ever seems to be necessary.

Use your majlis

The last element of active leadership is 'management by *majlis*'. As noted in Chapter 8, the *majlis* can take many forms, both informal and formal. Here we are concerned with meetings between the leaders and their advisers, in which problems are discussed and visions are created and shared. Management by *majlis* particularly focuses on creating a common understanding among the senior policymakers within an organization. It is a process of information sharing as well as reflection, a time to think out of the box as well as to build the box. It provides an opportunity for leadership to be truly active and creative.

Think about your own organization. Do you know your CEO's goals and key issues? Do you know your manager's goals and key issues? Do you actively and quickly share new information with senior leaders on their key issues? In Dubai, the answer to all these questions is invariably yes.

One example illustrates the effectiveness of the *majlis*. The Al Maha Desert Resort is an eco-tourism resort in the desert near Dubai. It's set within extensive desert grounds, enclosed to protect the endangered *al maha* (Arabian oryx, resembling antelopes) that roam freely on the grounds. Friends of the authors who were staying at this resort went on a guided wildlife tour. During the drive the guide noticed a hole in the fence and got on the radio to report the problem, suggesting that they had probably lost at least one *al maha*. Within 15 minutes of the call, Sheikh Mohammed himself was on the radio to the tour guide, asking questions and suggesting where to locate the animal. The wayward *al maha* was found where Sheikh Mohammed suspected it would be.

Think about the implications of this story. Someone hears about a development on an issue that is important to their leader, and the information filters through to the leader within minutes. What is interesting is not so much that this communication happens, but why it happens. Through the cascading communication that occurs via the *majlis,* the priorities of Sheikh Mohammed are widely known and his values are understood. So when an incident like this occurs, the people involved know that he would want to be informed, and his familiarity with the area allows him to be of immediate assistance.

Compare this with your own organization. Management by *majlis* is one key process for creating this shared understanding of what information to convey, and the other elements of active leadership create the trust for conveying the needed information. The performance implications of such a system are obvious. But think again about your own organization. How often do senior managers meet to reflect on strategy and share information and insights? Daily? Weekly? Monthly? Quarterly? Annually? Never? Can your organization afford not to change its habits?

Manage the cycle

As outlined earlier, the strategic trajectory model represents an iteration of asset creation (see diagram on the next page). Starting

Strategic trajectory

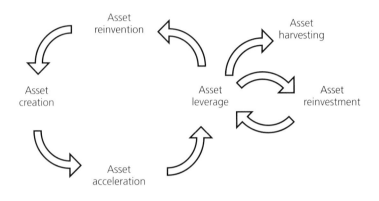

with the creation of a new asset from scratch, asset acceleration then acts as a coiling spring, ready to release the inherent value in the asset. Next is leverage, where innovation is spurred by competition among assets. To close the loop and complete the cycle, assets can then be harvested (retired), or reinvested or reinvented, in which case a new asset is created and the cycle begins again.

In managing this cycle, there are several imperatives: break free from limits, create assets strategically, set up corporate 'free zones', and know when to step back.

Break free from limits
When Dubai ran out of beach along its coastline, the government set about doubling it by building the Palms. Sheikh Mohammed turned the horse-training business on its head by establishing his training stables in Dubai and sponsoring the world's richest horse race. Dubai has filled its hotels nearly to capacity during the most inhospitable hot months of the year by developing attractions and clever marketing. The rulers of Dubai created a dynamic, modern, cosmopolitan city on a site that was desert only 50 years before. In the asset creation stage, starting with a blank slate may be daunting,

but it is also liberating. If you can see past the constraints, in terms of resources, finance or available time, it is possible to come up with radical strategies that set the stage for rapid growth. Of course, it's still important to keep the ultimate goals in mind, but if you can focus on what you want to achieve and work towards it, apart from the usual constraints, the assets (whether real or virtual) you create will power you along your strategic trajectory.

Create assets strategically

In order to create assets strategically, there must be a clearly articulated strategy or vision to guide your actions. Remembering that each asset (or initiative, project, acquisition and so on) becomes part of the larger strategic vortex, it is crucial to ensure that each new introduction will add to the overall value and growth of the ecosystem, not languish on its own or, worse still, suck valuable resources from other parts of the vortex.

Dubai is full of examples of how this has been done. The country was already a recognized trading centre early in the 20th century, so it made perfect sense to build on that awareness using the expertise and resources of the local population and visiting traders. Thus the Creek was dredged, Port Rashid was built, Jebel Ali was created and other assets followed to further support this strategy. The strategy changed over time, branching out to create local bases for traders in the free zones and developing intermodal transport facilities as air travel became economically attractive. The addition of each asset in this group has been highly strategic, each focusing on furthering Dubai's position as a trading hub. Within the context of related aspects of the vision, other examples include the development of tourism and the transition to a knowledge-based economy. All of these strands of the vision work together and play off each other. As a result, there are few businesses in Dubai that seem isolated from a commonly recognized vision and that provide little economic value added.

The lessons from this are clear and readily applicable elsewhere.

First, make sure the vision of your organization is clear and commonly understood. Then be certain that every major new initiative, project or acquisition is making a solid contribution to that vision, driving the organization in the right direction. Failure to do this can lead to the business becoming fragmented and unfocused, a position from which it is difficult to get back on track.

Set up corporate free zones …
The free zone concept, under which investors who set up inside the zones enjoy substantially more freedom to trade and manage their businesses and finances than they would anywhere else in the region, is not a new idea in Dubai.

The largest free zone, Jebel Ali, was set up in the 1980s, but it can be argued that the airport was the first when it was established with an open-skies policy in 1960. The free zone model has more recently been extended to Dubai Internet City, Dubai Media City, Dubai Silicon Oasis and Dubai International Financial Centre. It is a beautifully simple concept and an important part of the asset acceleration phase in the strategic trajectory model. In a corporate context, though, can you create an environment within your company where there is minimal bureaucracy, where you invite the world in and where you actively benchmark the rest of the world? Or do you continue to compare yourself with the same five companies at arm's length, doing the same things every quarter?

When a state opens itself to the world, the resulting interaction works as a supercluster, a supercharged microcosm of global competition. This competition sets representatives from all corners of the globe against one another, not just one primary industry in one area as you see in Silicon Valley or Solingen, a region in Germany where many of the world's best knives are made. When this happens, the amount of innovation increases by orders of magnitude because of the sheer diversity and range of inputs. And everyone's a winner: the innovative companies, their customers, the industry and the host that brought them all together and turned up the heat.

… and one-stop shops

Another important element of the free zone concept is the idea of the 'one-stop shop'. This term may be a cliché, but it's exactly how the managers of the free zones in Dubai describe it. It's a single point of contact within the zone, where any and all questions, support issues, administrative needs and other problems can be addressed. In a business environment, the equivalent might be a 'corporate concierge', which can serve the same function on an organizational level when enabled with a charter or clear understanding and guidelines from the central office or parent corporation.

Global clusters

The idea behind economic geography or clustering is that when competing firms locate in a small geographic area, innovation increases and results in more efficient transfer of knowledge and continuous improvement in best practices.

Examples of clustering include the high-tech firms of Silicon Valley, mechanical watch making in Switzerland and clothing manufacturing in northern Italy. The basic idea behind clusters is that when competing firms locate in a small geographic area innovation increases because of increased competition and the more efficient transfer of knowledge and best practices through employee turnover.

Dubai has taken the concept to another level as part of the process of asset acceleration and leverage. In creating free zones, Dubai announced that it was an open house to the world. So instead of creating regional clusters, it created global clusters, with the entire world competing in a small space. This enables even greater innovation because more firms are competing. And because UAE nationals work alongside skilled expatriates in the zones, the local workers benefit from the knowledge and best practices that companies from all over the world have to offer.

The lesson for corporations is clear. When establishing major new initiatives, learn from the world, not just a few local or usual competitors. This is the only way to ensure long-run globally competitive businesses.

Corporate concierge

For virtually any problem, question or requirement that comes up for a company inside one of the Dubai free zones, there is a single point of contact within the zone that can address it. This bundle of corporate concierge services is the catalyst that has provided much of the accelerated value in the free zones.

In the development of Dubai Internet City and Dubai Media City, the concierge service guaranteed the procurement of work permits within 24 hours. In addition, it resolved any business or logistical questions. To further enhance customer service, the corporate concierge handles non-business issues, embracing total customer care through providing contacts for relocating employees seeking housing and schooling for children. And, taking the corporate concierge concept yet another step further, the management of these free zones helps market the companies located there through road trips and trade shows.

Turning to the lessons that can be learnt from this, ask yourself a couple of questions. How easy is it for outsiders to do business with your company? Do you actively facilitate this process or are you a necessary evil that they must work through?

In today's highly competitive business environment, establishing a corporate concierge service for dealing with outside companies may be one way to improve competitiveness through differentiation and better customer service. Corporations must identify the services that their customers want, and then explore the cost/benefit ratio of providing these services. A single point of contact – a corporate concierge – can be of immense value in getting close to customers and in learning what their needs are.

As seen in the free zones of Dubai, much of the value created by the corporate concierge service was focused inwardly, providing value to the companies within them. In a business environment, this concept may be reminiscent of the shared service centre, but it is really much more. Shared services in corporations rarely exhibit the proactive spirit that Dubai's corporate concierge services seem to. They want companies to succeed and thus do whatever they can to enable that, whether that means engaging in marketing activities or taking on responsibility for administrative tasks and red tape.

Instead of becoming a backwater of back-office tasks, the corporate concierge inside a business can be a strong enabler, allowing managers to focus on their business. Such a service can also become a powerful catalyst for cross-pollination, helping to create synergies between business units and building bridges between silos.

Know when to step back

The asset leverage phase of the strategic trajectory model in Dubai has been successful largely because the leaders know when to step back and let competition flourish, thereby encouraging innovation and rapid growth. At the same time, however, it's important to keep an eye on things to know when adjustments or even major changes are needed.

There are many examples of how the leadership has stepped back in Dubai. In the hotel industry, for example, new hotels are constantly being built, each with its own innovative qualities and superlative characteristics. The exploding demand for office space in Dubai Internet City and Dubai Media City is another good example. Demand has exceeded all expectations and has enabled development of a wide range of properties within the Technology, Electronic Commerce and Media Free Zone, including more offices, residential units and leisure facilities.

It can be difficult to loosen your grip on a project, particularly when you have been intimately involved in its development. But an active leader should be confident that the vision that's been communicated is sufficient to guide free growth and development with little intervention. Timing matters, of course. When is the right time to step back? There is not a simple answer to this question. In order to make an informed decision, managers must have access to a range of timely, accurate and complete information. Access to this information is crucial throughout the strategic trajectory. Ways to make this happen are addressed in the next section.

Lubricate the system

Once asset leverage has taken place, choosing whether to reinvest, reinvent or harvest will be based on an organization's project assessment criteria, which will encompass elements of its vision and strategy, financial performance indicators, and systems.

We have looked at several examples of how leaders in Dubai have 'closed the loop' by reinvesting, reinventing or harvesting assets as part of the strategic trajectory of individual assets or groups of assets, while also contributing to the cultivation of the larger strategic vortex. Existing centres of expertise in the Police Academy and the Ports Authority have been reinvented as new offerings for customers outside Dubai. We have examined many examples of reinvestment, such as in Dubai's infrastructure, noting in particular how continual reinvestment in commercial office space and other areas has raised standards markedly in the past decade. We also saw that, although there are examples of asset harvesting, there is a tendency to reinvent before the point of harvesting can be reached.

Making decisions on reinvestment, reinvention and harvesting successfully depends on good information flows and effective lines of communication. More fundamentally, it depends on maintaining focus on the vision and its key objectives. The implications of some of these success factors as they can be applied in any organization are discussed below.

Keep it simple
Organizational structures in Dubai, both in the government and in

the private sector, are remarkably simple. One reason things can happen as quickly as they do is that there is little distance between the bottom and the top of organizations. Open-door policies give every employee direct access to senior managers, who invariably have direct access to the rulers. This openness and few levels of hierarchy, combined with the tendency of managers to get involved in the daily lives of their subordinates, paints a clear picture of how communication happens and how things get done.

Simplicity is at the heart of Dubai's approach that 'what's good for business is good for Dubai', down to the micro level of a single business traveller and the spillover economic effects that he creates during his stay through the money he spends in hotels, restaurants and shops, and through the business he does.

One reason Dubai's ruling family has been successful is that even with the rapid development of recent years, government has been kept lean and lines of communication open. In the corporate context, better communication can be achieved by flattening layers of management and ensuring that leaders are visible and accessible, both for the reasons already outlined and to ensure that they keep abreast of what is happening. The less complex the organizational structure, the easier it will be for management to become aware of problems and strategic issues and to take appropriate action. It also makes it easier for management to recognize the true strengths of the organization and to exploit them.

In Dubai, massive projects have been conceived, planned and built in a seemingly impossible timeframe. This hasn't been achieved by cutting corners; the unusually high standards in Dubai are a result of the country's ability to attract the best minds and hands. Time is usually saved in the planning process. As long as the feasibility has been proven, there's nothing wrong with starting before it's clear how everything will be done. But this does require careful attention to detail and frequent monitoring, so that potential problems can be identified and avoided or corrected before they do any damage.

For most organizations, one of the biggest difficulties in the planning process is in getting decisions made, particularly about allocation of resources. The question for most organizations is can the process be speeded up? This generally comes down to how can the corporate culture be made freer and more trusting? Returning to one of Sheikh Mohammed's favourite analogies: as long as you're running, even if you fall you'll fall forward, and when you get up, you'll still be making progress. And if you're running along with your colleagues, they'll be there to help you get up and keep going.

Stick to the vision and core values

An uncomplicated organizational structure and clear lines of communication allow action to be taken quickly, which is particularly important when problems arise or things become tricky. But how do you decide what action to take? In Dubai it has been shown that it usually makes sense to stick to your original vision despite problems arising. That is the reason Emirates decided not to reduce its $15 billion order for aircraft following the slump in air travel after the 2001 terrorist attacks on New York and Washington.

Dubai's leaders have managed to create a sense of confidence in the emirate's innate strengths that has encouraged the belief that Dubai can survive virtually any downturn or slump. Compare this attitude with that of many companies today which make cuts when faced with the slightest hint of trouble. Of course, quoted companies have to keep their investors happy and provide returns in the short term as well as the long term, but a robust, flexible vision can help accommodate their wishes while providing a roadmap to navigate any trouble spots that arise.

Don't be afraid to blur boundaries

Many of the senior government officials in Dubai also run businesses and head other organizations. This has provided a direct communication channel between business and government and therefore enabled rapid and effective responsiveness. This direct communication conduit is very important in the reinvestment and reinvention phases of the strategic trajectory model. Messages get to decision-makers fast, so assets can be reinvented or harvested, keeping to the vision.

In the corporate context, managers often work for head office or for a business unit and not on both sides of the fence. This often results in an 'us and them' culture, when what organizations really need is a straightforward 'us' culture. Managers who can represent the interests of their business units as well as those of the head office will develop an ability to think and act globally, which can only benefit the corporation.

Cultivate the ecosystem

The strategic vortex is composed of multiple cycles of the strategic trajectory (see diagram on next page). Strategies build one on top of the other. Taking a step back, it's easy to see how this has been effective in Dubai. The rulers started with the Creek and some traders. The Creek was developed and an airport was built to bring in more trade and businessmen. Because no one would want to stay in Dubai if there were no reliable roads, or water and electricity supplies, they built those too. Then came oil and some real money, which was put to work improving the facilities. More ports and some heavy industry ensured that Dubai didn't go unnoticed. To satisfy the businessmen who were coming in greater numbers, the World Trade Centre and some good hotels were built. To bring even more people and more freight, Emirates was set up. This removed reliance on foreign airlines and made Dubai more self-sufficient, and virtually guaranteed a constant influx of travellers and goods. To help companies using the ports to do some value-added manufacturing, a free zone next to the biggest port was created. The businesses in Dubai Internet City and Media City are attracting a new calibre of worker, who demands good leisure and

Strategic vortex

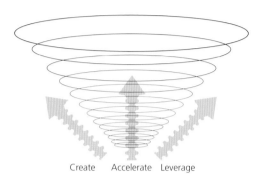

Create   Accelerate   Leverage

healthcare facilities and the right to own property, so projects are being developed to satisfy those needs. For all this to work, robust capital and financial services markets are needed, so the Dubai International Financial Centre is given the go-ahead.

Each strategy builds on the base of the previous one, thus expanding the strategic vortex.

In a corporate context, the lesson from Dubai is that you should decide where you're going and pull out all the stops to get there, building on one strength to take you to the next, still monitoring and adjusting at each step.

Use core competencies with care

In recent decades, there has been a shift in how we think about the sources of competitive advantage. In the 1980s, industry structure was considered to be at the heart of competitive advantage.[2] In the 1990s, the essence of competitive advantage was thought to be characteristics internal to the firm, such as resources, competencies, knowledge and capabilities.[3] This transition was caused by two main factors.

☐ **The pace of change.** Industries are moving so quickly that industry snapshots of the competitive landscape are no longer relevant by the time the strategy based on them is implemented. Increasingly, what is required is continuing analysis or videotape.

☐ **The blurring of industry boundaries.** An industry-based view of strategy depends on being able to clearly define the industry, but convergence is making this increasingly difficult. This has massive implications, as drivers of profits are often based on the number of competitors, the relative sizes of these competitors and other factors. This sense of convergence increases in industries affected by information technology. Consider the media wars (internet versus print), device wars (cell phones with digital cameras or PDAs) and information wars (retail loyalty cards allow access to vast amounts of customer information, which is often the key to accessing new markets, such as retail financial services).

As a result there has been a massive shift in how firms think about strategy, and many have jumped on the core competencies bandwagon. It's almost impossible to pick up a business publication nowadays without reading about a divestiture or acquisition being justified by the core competencies. Companies are either ridding themselves of 'non-core assets' or 'acquiring core assets'.

However, in reacting to the financially motivated diversification logic of earlier decades, many companies may have taken the idea of core competencies too far. In recent years, more and more firms have entered into outsourcing and alliance relationships as they attempt to streamline their unwieldy businesses in order to be more responsive to turbulent environments. As a result of this streamlining, many firms are now focusing on one or two core competencies as their source of competitive advantage.

But what will happen to those companies that have narrowly defined themselves around a single core competence when the

Limitations of core competencies

world no longer values that core competence? In other words, are there limits to the applicability of the idea of core competencies?

One of the findings of the authors' research in Dubai suggests that environmental uncertainty may be a good reason for firms to expand their core competencies and activities (see diagram above). In times of uncertainty, following a core competence logic may result in missing opportunities, whereas if your range of competence is broader you have more balls to juggle and potentially more opportunities to take advantage of.

Given that the advantages or disadvantages of a core competence focus may depend on the level of uncertainty of the business environment, the diagram above indicates that the 'sweet spot' for companies using core competencies as their primary form of strategic thinking is medium levels of uncertainty. The recent high-tech fallout reinforces this concept. Narrowly pursuing a single skill set is a dangerous and often fatal activity in turbulent competitive environments.

As well as environmental uncertainty, the authors' research in Dubai revealed a second factor limiting the applicability of core competencies: the extent of market development and reliability.

Following a narrowly defined business strategy based on one or two core competencies has an immediate result for a firm: all non-core or non-essential activities are carried out externally through contractual relationships (outsourcing) or strategic partnerships and alliances. Such a strategy is only possible if the market in which the firm is competing is reasonably mature and has a host of capable firms to handle these transactions. If not, the firm cannot outsource these activities and must pursue a less narrowly defined strategy.

There is one further dimension to the argument about the limitation of core competencies. In the case of Dubai, it was initially at a competitive disadvantage in respect of more developed countries. In order to accelerate growth, it invited the world to compete through its free zones. However, if firms invite other world-class firms into their markets to facilitate long-term growth and learning, how do they survive in the short to medium term? In many cases, narrowly pursuing one or two core competencies may not be the best answer.

Instead, it is advisable to have a superstructure in place to capture the externalities or spillover benefits of those transactions. 'Superstructure' refers to the extended local business ecosystem in which these firms operate. In Dubai, the superstructure that helped these firms thrive included the restaurants, shops and other service industries that already existed when they set up shop in the emirate.

Dubai's superstructure can be compared to the Korean *chaebol* (large, diversified trading houses) and some of the large family businesses in India, such as the Birla or Tata groups. Why do these hugely diversified conglomerates exist, producing everything from high-tech to white goods to shipping to automobiles? Is there a model here that suggests that in certain types of environments, at a certain stage of industry and country-market evolution, these large, diversified companies make sense? The strategic vortex model of asset creation, acceleration and leverage is evidence that they do reap the benefits of new companies entering.

These companies are not pursuing a strategy of unrelated

diversification. Instead, the diversification strategy of the customer interacts within the whole business ecosystem. For example, there is a famous story in Dubai about Sheikh Rashid, Sheikh Mohammed's father, who was asked why he was building an airport in Dubai, even if it was only a refuelling centre. He said:

> If a person lands in Dubai, he will take a taxi, buy a pack of cigarettes, have a meal, and we will benefit.

This is why Dubai has built the superstructure of activities to facilitate the tourism industry: world-class hotels, restaurants, transportation, safety and so on. For businesses, Dubai has created the superstructure necessary for rapid growth. Innovative projects such as Dubai Internet City and Dubai Media City require many of the same things as the tourism industry, but as the number of companies increases, they also require financial markets (hence the Dubai Financial Market and the Dubai International Financial Centre), healthcare (enter Healthcare City) and eventually a sense of permanence and belonging (foreigners can now own property in certain areas of Dubai). Again, the expanding superstructure captures the set of related activities needed to service major segments of customer needs.

For corporations, this raises a similar question. What set of activities is needed to service major segments of related customer needs? Customer-activity related diversification differs from the traditional definition of diversification in terms of competencies, products or geographic markets. Such customer-activity related diversification is one way non-market leaders or developing corporations – that is, most corporations – may gain a competitive advantage.

Conclusion

It's easy to arrive in Dubai or pick up a newspaper article about the emirate and immediately see evidence of the progress that's been made. The skyscrapers, the airport and ports, the thriving tourism industry and projects like the Palm Islands all illustrate what has been achieved in recent years. Where less than 50 years ago there was little more than sand, silicon chips will soon be produced and distributed all over the world.

As we have tried to make clear in this book, the real successes of Dubai are not so much the outward evidence but more the culture and spirit that have allowed the world-class assets to be created and spun into a strategic vortex that can continue to grow and expand. Dubai's leadership has taken the risk of inviting individuals and investors from all over the world to help contribute to this success. In the process, a tolerant, varied culture has been created. Just as the diversified assets within the strategic vortex make it more robust, so too does the diversity of Dubai's culture allow it to continue to develop. It's no coincidence that expatriates in many Middle Eastern countries complete their two- or three-year assignments and then move on, but many of those who are posted to Dubai on a temporary assignment decide to remain. Dubai retains its traditional cultural and religious beliefs, but it also embraces those of the many individuals and groups that make up its population, allowing every resident to feel at home and at ease.

The risks inherent in a population in which four out of every five residents are foreign are significant, but Dubai's leadership has recognized that bringing the world into the emirate will allow it to compete more effectively on an international scale. The social fabric of Dubai has become one of its most valuable resources, and that's not something that can be built as easily as a skyscraper or a luxury hotel. It takes leadership, vision, open-mindedness and patience.

The challenge to organizations is to create a diverse, pluralistic, inclusive culture that can not only support the growth of the concern, but also prove an irresistible attraction to customers and potential employees. We have referred to vision repeatedly in this book: the vision we're talking about must be able to keep people focused on the same strategic trajectory while allowing individual cultures and perspectives to thrive.

When a traveller arrives in Dubai its diversity and multiculturalism is immediately visible, as is the underlying spirit, enthusiasm and positive attitude of its people. After leaving, it is this spirit that remains most memorable. How can you create the same spirit within your organization, one that remains with your customers independently of the products and services you may have offered them? Going global usually means setting up offices around the world. But what if you were to start by bringing the world into your organization instead?

For the creation and cultivation of the strategic vortex that allows rapid growth, this kind of underlying culture is essential, as is a vision that's flexible, inclusive and, ultimately, liberating.

Notes

1 The skunk-works methodology is based on the assembly of an ad hoc project team to address a problem without the traditional organizational trappings being imposed on it. Famously first used at Lockheed in the 1940s, where it is now known as the 'Lockheed Martin Advanced Development Program'. The commonly accepted etymology for the term cites Al Capp's *L'il Abner* comic strip, where 'Big Barnsmell's Skonk Works' is a still used to produce a bootleg liquor called Chicago JoyJuice.

2 *Competitive Strategy* (Porter, M. 1980: Free Press, New York) is an often-cited source for this type of thinking

3 In general, this is known as the resource-based school of strategy. Influential works in this area include Prahalad, C.K. and Hamel, G. 1990. The Core Competence of the Corporation. *Harvard Business Review*, 68(3), pp. 79–91; and Barney, J.B. 1991. Firm Resources and Sustained Competitive Advantage. *Journal of Management*, Vol. 17, pp. 99–120

Postscript

As we reflect on the story of Dubai and its implications for corporations and countries, we are struck that even after all the success that Dubai has achieved, many challenges still remain and, indeed, many more will evolve in keeping with the accelerated pace of development.

Any time a company or country goes through rapid change, there is invariably a tendency to cling to the past, not necessarily in terms of business practices, but more in terms of culture and practices – this may even be more true for a country which may be older with potentially more entrenched behaviour. Thus, we suggest for Dubai, as well as companies that have gone through such a rapid transformation, that the challenges ahead may be as daunting as the ones just gone through.

In order to succeed in the times ahead, it is necessary to remember what enabled this country to change in the first place – desire: a desire to better their current situation or standing, initially regionally, and now within the global economy. In the process of pursuing its ambition, Dubai became a hotbed of ideas and people from around the world, and government-led financing often kick-started these visions into becoming reality. The artful mixing of these elements, and the managing of the accompanying risk, has proved a powerful recipe for success.

Today is no different for Dubai. In order to succeed, it will need to continue to be, albeit more so, a primary market for ideas, people, and capital. Unfortunately, the desire to change is often less when the current degree of success is relatively high. The expectations of the new stakeholders in the economy may challenge the pace of change. Social, economic and political norms will be challenged, as already is happening. The challenges to leadership in steering Dubai forward will be even greater, as the ship continues to grow larger. Crucial will be the ability to minimize bureaucracy, thus enabling speed, while simultaneously ensuring equity is not compromised for the broader set of stakeholders in the new economy.

Again, companies should reflect on the challenges facing Dubai and learn for themselves. Companies are the nexus of ideas, people, and capital – the catalyst in the recipe. Attracting and retaining these elements is the key to success. The challenge for senior management is to create a culture and leadership style that will keep the organization growing, no matter what its past success. Easy to say, but it is something that few have been able to achieve.

Let us all look to Dubai over the next few years to see, if again, it can provide insights in how to achieve this sustained rapid growth.

Appendix 1 Timeline

Year	Event
1820	Britain establishes presence in the Gulf, with the first of several truce agreements, making the region known as the Trucial Coast
1833	Group of Bani Yas tribe settles in Dubai, led by Al Maktoum family
1892	Agreement is signed giving Britain control of foreign affairs of Trucial Coast
1903	UK steamships begin calling at Dubai
1912	Sheikh Saeed Bin Maktoum becomes ruler
1930s	Worldwide depression and introduction of Japanese cultured pearls starts decline of Dubai pearling trade
1930s	Population of Dubai is 20,000
1950s	First oil is discovered in the Trucial States
1952	Electricity is introduced
1958	Sheikh Saeed dies, and Sheikh Rashid Bin Saeed Al Maktoum becomes ruler
1959	First hotel opens in Dubai
1960	Dredging of Dubai Creek is completed
1960	Dubai International Airport opens
1962	Oil production begins in neighbouring Abu Dhabi
1963	Al Maktoum Bridge over Dubai Creek is completed
1963	National Bank of Dubai is established
1966	Oil is discovered in Dubai
1968	UK announces its intention to withdraw from region
1969	First oil exports from Dubai
1971	United Arab Emirates (UAE) is founded

1971	UAE joins the Arab League
1971	UAE joins the United Nations
1972	Port Rashid opens with 15 berths
1975	Population of Dubai is 183,200
1978	Port Rashid is expanded to 35 berths
1979	Jebel Ali Port is opened
1979	Dubai Dry Docks is established
1979	Dubai Aluminium Company (DUBAL) begins operations
1979	Dubai International Trade Centre is completed (later called the Dubai World Trade Centre)
1980	2.8 million passengers use Dubai International Airport
1981	UAE is founding member of the Gulf Co-operation Council (GCC)
1985	Jebel Ali Free Zone opens
1985	Emirates Airline is founded
1989	First Dubai Desert Classic, part of the PGA European Tour
1989	First Dubai Air Show
1990	632,903 people visit Dubai (based on number of hotel guests)
1990	Sheikh Rashid dies, his son Sheikh Maktoum Bin Rashid Al Maktoum becomes ruler
1990	5 million passengers use Dubai International Airport
1995	Population of Dubai is 690,400
1995	Sheikh Mohammed becomes Crown Prince
1995	120 nationalities are present in Dubai
1996	First Dubai Shopping Festival
1996	First running of the Dubai World Cup horse race
1997	Emaar Properties is established
1997	Department of Tourism and Commerce Marketing is established
1999	Burj Al Arab hotel is completed
1999	Residential property developments are announced open to non-GCC nationals to buy

2000	Dubai Financial Market is established
2000	2.8 million people visit Dubai (based on number of hotel guests)
2000	Dubai Internet City opens
2000	12.3 passengers use Dubai International Airport
2001	Dubai Media City opens
2001	First Dubai Strategy Forum meeting
2001	Construction on Palm Jumeirah begins
2002	Dubai Metals and Commodities Centre is established
2002	Dubai International Financial Centre is announced
2002	Dubai's e-government website is launched
2002	Dubai Silicon Oasis is announced
2002	First sale of land to non-GCC nationals (30–35 plots sold in Mirdif)
2003	203 nationalities are present in Dubai
2003	Dubai hosts annual meetings of the boards of governors of the World Bank Group and International Monetary Fund

Appendix 2 GDP

Gross domestic product, 2001 (current prices)

	——— $ million ———		— % of non-oil total —	
	Dubai	UAE	Dubai	UAE
Total	17,518	67,114	–	–
Non-oil sectors	16,026	48,289	100.0	100.0
Agriculture & fisheries	141	2,622	0.9	5.4
Mining & quarrying	20	188	0.1	0.4
Manufacturing	2,820	9,306	17.6	19.3
Electricity & water	294	1,322	1.8	2.7
Construction	1,422	4,715	8.9	9.8
Trade	2,866	6,172	17.9	12.8
Hotels & restaurants	782	1,464	4.9	3.0
Transport, storage & communications	2,328	4,855	14.5	10.1
Finance & insurance	1,919	4,568	12.0	9.5
Real estate	1,714	5,314	10.7	11.0
Government services	1,618	7,434	10.1	15.4
Other services	598	1,562	3.7	3.2
Less: imputed bank services	−496	−1,234	−3.1	−2.6

GDP per head, 2001 ($)

	Dubai
GDP (total)	19,244
Non-oil GDP	17,605

Dubai: GDP real growth rates

	1996	1997*	1998*	1999*	2000*	2001†
GDP	7.0	5.5	5.3	8.2	7.5	4.0
Non-oil GDP	10.9	12.1	5.3	9.2	8.9	4.8

* Adjusted
† Preliminary

NOTE ON SOURCE USED FOR APPENDICES

Statistics and sources for Appendices 2–8 were taken from Department of Economic Development, *Development Statistics of Dubai, 2002*. The currency was converted at the rate of Dh3.67 per US$1.

Appendix 3 Population

Dubai: population ('000)

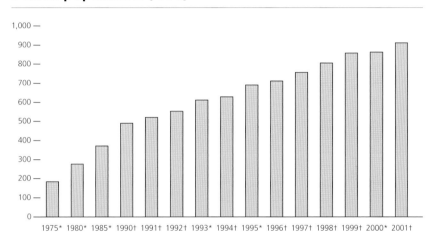

* Final results of population census   † Mid-year estimates

Source: Ministry of Planning and Dubai Municipality

Appendix 4 Employment

Dubai: employment by economic sectors

	—— 1990 ——		—— 2001* ——	
	No.	%	No.	%
Total	205,558	–	594,159	–
Non-oil sectors	204,297	100.0	590,479	100.0
Agriculture	3,949	1.9	8,148	1.4
Mining & quarrying	365	0.2	698	0.1
Manufacturing	22,980	11.2	94,132	15.9
Electricity & water	4,636	2.3	6,470	1.1
Construction	26,715	13.1	90,432	15.3
Trade	44,750	21.9	144,296	24.4
Restaurants & hotels	10,315	5.0	34,255	5.8
Transport, storage & communication	22,702	11.1	41,720	7.1
Finance, insurance	5,940	2.9	12,602	2.1
Real estate & businesss services	6,059	3.0	17,297	2.9
Government services	28,118	13.8	52,900	9.0
Other services	27,768	13.6	87,579	14.8

* Preliminary
Source: Ministry of Planning

Appendix 5 Trade

Dubai: non-oil foreign trade

	——— $ million ———		——— '000 Tonnes ———	
	2000	*2001*	*2000*	*2001*
Imports	19,725	22,667	11,037	11,428
Exports	1,489	1,610	1,347	1,570
Re-exports	4,812	6,151	2,373	2,465
Total trade	26,026	30,428	14,757	15,463

Main types of imports, 2001

		$ million	*%*
1	Live animals, animal products	388	1.7
2	Vegetable products	898	4.0
3	Animal and vegetable fats, oils and waxes	44	0.2
4	Prepared foodstuff, beverages, tobacco	558	2.5
5	Mineral products	180	0.8
6	Products of chemical or allied industries	1,244	5.5
7	Plastics, rubber and rubber articles	829	3.7
8	Raw hides, skins, leather, etc and articles	132	0.6
9	Wood, cork, plaiting materials and articles	228	1.0
10	Wood pulp, paper products, waste paper	275	1.2
11	Textiles and textile articles	2,527	11.1
12	Footwear, headgear, umbrellas, etc	239	1.1
13	Articles of stone, cement, asbestos, ceramics, glass	447	2.0
14	Pearls, precious stones and metals	4,353	19.2
15	Base metals and base metals articles	1,568	6.3
16	Machinery, sound recorders, TV, etc	4,861	21.4
17	Vehicles, aircraft, vessels, etc	2,795	12.3
18	Optical, medical, etc equipment, watches	611	2.7
19	Arms and ammunition, parts and accessories	2	0.0
20	Miscellaneous manufactured articles	620	2.7
21	Art work, collectors pieces and antiques	5	0.0
	Total	22,667	100.0

Source: Ports, Customs and Free Zone Corporation

Main sources of imports

	2000		2001	
	$ million	*%*	*$ million*	*%*
China	1,945	9.9	2,110	9.3
UK	1,518	7.7	1,610	7.1
Japan	1,622	8.2	1,568	6.9
India	1,446	7.3	1,563	6.9
USA	1,325	6.7	1,562	6.9
Switzerland	238	1.2	1,513	6.7
Germany	1,027	5.2	1,392	6.1
France	1,424	7.2	1,295	5.7
South Korea	1,198	6.1	1,274	5.6
Italy	930	4.7	927	4.1

Appendix 6 Transport

Arrivals and departures at Dubai International Airport

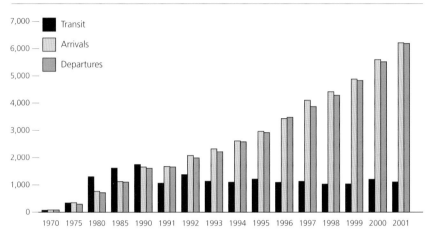

Source: Department of Civil Aviation

Air cargo handled at Dubai International Airport, ('000 tonnes)

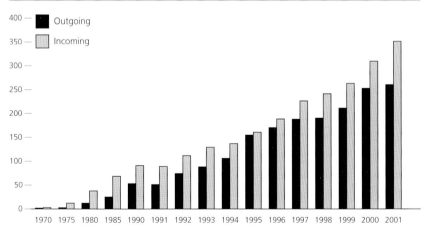

Source: Department of Civil Aviation

Vessels calling at Port Rashid and Jebel Ali

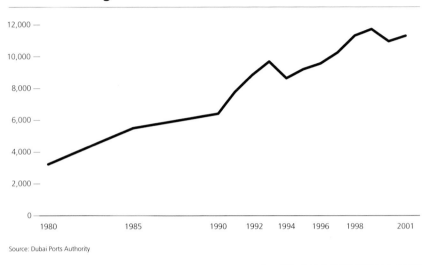

Source: Dubai Ports Authority

Total cargo handled at Port Rashid and Jebel Ali ('000 tonnes)

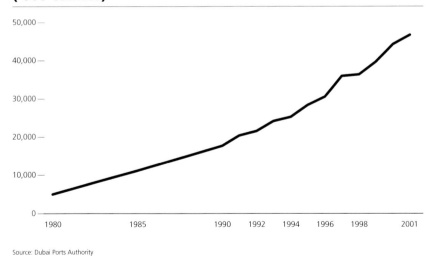

Source: Dubai Ports Authority

Motor vehicles registered at Dubai

	Cars	Buses & trucks	Motor cycles	Others	Total
1990	20,823	4,107	271	241	25,622
1991	23,305	4,378	247	491	28,421
1992	28,276	5,239	388	479	34,382
1993	28,257	5,506	453	649	34,865
1994	26,339	5,811	525	796	33,471
1995	23,626	5,331	534	683	30,174
1996	29,431	626	623	5,738	36,418
1997	41,343	953	674	2,157	45,127
1998	45,094	5,929	818	3,616	55,457
1999	47,181	1,307	791	1,186	50,465
2000	50,216	622	796	2,711	54,345
2001	75,907	2,227	1,165	9,877	89,176

Source: Dubai Police General HQ

Appendix 7 Construction

Dubai: completed buildings

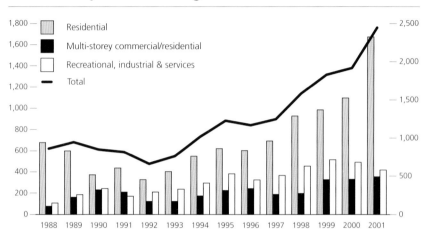

Source: Dubai Municipality

Dubai: land transactions

	Number	$ million
1970	630	9
1975	1,607	219
1980	491	82
1985	804	973
1990	1,400	463
1991	1,271	402
1992	1,832	746
1993	2,383	1,279
1994	1,857	1,299
1995	1,541	873
1996	1,897	1,837
1997	2,510	2,223
1998	2,291	2,328
1999	3,558	1,779
2000	2,636	1,564
2001	3,201	2,345

Source: Lands Department

Appendix 8 Hotels and tourism

Dubai: number of hotels*

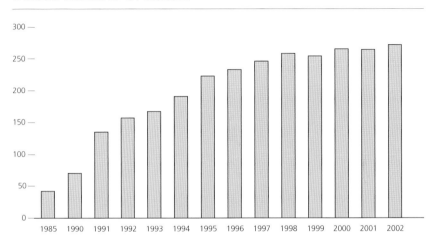

*Excluding hotels planned or under construction.
Sources: Ministry of Planning (1985–94); Department of Economic Development (1995–8);
Department of Tourism and Commerce Marketing (after 1998)

Dubai: hotel guests by nationality (%)

	1985	1990	1995	2002
UAE	4.7	5.8	5.6	7.0
GCC	17.4	19.4	22.1	20.0
Other Arab	9.2	7.9	6.3	10.0
Other Asian & African	36.7	39.7	25.8	22.0
European	28.8	23.9	35.5	28.0
American	3.0	3.1	4.2	5.0
Oceanic	0.3	0.2	0.5	2.0

Dubai: guest nights by nationality (%)

	1985	1990	1995	2001
UAE	3.4	3.9	3.7	4.7
GCC	13.8	23.6	17.2	17.0
Other Arab	10.1	7.5	5.7	9.1
Other Asian & African	35.5	34.2	23.8	26.7
European	32.4	27.6	45.6	37.9
American	4.3	3.1	3.4	3.5
Oceanic	0.7	0.2	0.5	1.1

Dubai: hotel rooms and occupancy rates

	Deluxe	First class	Second class	Others	Total
Hotel rooms, no.					
1985	3,040	1,200	287	74	4,601
1990	2,901	1,100	556	821	5,378
1991	2,926	1,128	592	1,530	6,176
1992	2,994	1,191	1,140	2,889	8,214
1993	3,265	1,793	1,457	2,868	9,383
1994	3,616	2,037	1,485	3,266	10,404
1995	4,796	2,114	2,040	3,777	12,727
1996	4,873	2,394	2,029	4,023	13,319
1997	5,354	2,757	2,084	4,028	14,223
1998	7,270	3,288	2,460	4,028	17,046
1999	8,364	4,225	2,636	3,413	18,638
2000	–	–	–	–	20,315
2001	–	–	–	–	21,428
Rooms occupancy rates, %					
1985	54.3	55.4	44.9	39.2	53.7
1990	69.9	63.6	58.1	42.3	63.2
1991	68.3	59.4	56.1	45.4	59.8
1992	70.1	59.8	47.5	36.2	53.6
1993	71.4	57.9	58.2	39.1	56.9
1994	70.5	62.2	62.1	47.5	60.5
1995	69.6	62.2	63.0	55.5	63.1
1996	73.9	66.4	65.0	59.2	66.8
1997	71.2	65.0	62.0	57.6	64.8
1998	63.5	59.9	56.7	50.5	58.7
1999	66.4	58.6	50.8	48.0	62.0
2000	–	–	–	–	61.2
2001	–	–	–	–	60.9

Index

Figures in bold indicate bar charts, line graphs and tables in Appendices; those in italics indicate illustrations in the text.